The Collector's Handbook

Tax Planning, Strategy and Estate Advice for Collectors and Their Heirs

James L. Halperin and Gregory J. Rohan

Edited by
Noah Fleisher, Brian Keagy,
Steve Lansdale and Steve Roach

IvyPress, Inc.

Dallas, Texas

By James L. Halperin and Gregory J. Rohan

Edited for 2023 by Brian Keagy and Steve Lansdale.

This publication is designed to provide accurate and authoritative information with respect to the subject matter covered. It is provided with the understanding that neither the authors nor the publisher are engaged in rendering legal, accounting, or other professional advice. If legal advice or other expert assistance is required, you should seek the services of a competent professional.

Choose the members of your financial team wisely, and don't be afraid to pay for good advice; it will save you money in the long run. You will likely need a CPA, a lawyer, a financial planner, and an insurance agent to execute the planning recommended in this book. Encourage your entire team to work together; a financial plan is only as good as it is holistic. Please remember that tax planning is an ongoing process and not an annual event. Collectors have special needs, and tax laws affect different collectors differently.

ISBN: 978-1-63351-472-0

Manufactured in the United States of America
© 2023, Revised Edition

Copyright Cover Design by Jonathan Fehr, 2023

A True Collector's Mentality

"My wish is, so that my drawings, my prints, my curiosities, my books, in a word, those things of Art which have been the joy of my life shall not be consigned to the cold tomb of a museum, and subjected to the stupid glance of the careless passer-by; but I require that they shall all be dispersed under the hammer of the auctioneer, so that the pleasure which the acquiring of each one has given to me, shall be given again, in each case, to some inheritor of my own tastes."

From the will of Edmond de Goncourt, 1896

"To those of us in the business of helping remove obstacles from the financial paths of clients, *The Collector's Handbook* is a valuable resource I would think that any advisor would want to have in their library."
- Jeffrey Turner, Certified Financial Planner™ professional,
President of Chattanooga Estate Planning Council

"A wealth of sound and practical information, written in a clear and concise manner. Must reading for every collector!"
– Leroy Van Allen, Numismatic Author and Morgan Dollar Expert

"…It is for everyone in numismatics and is even a 'must have' for those who may become heirs, but lack the know-how of what to do next. Senior citizens, like myself, will be especially happy with the interesting stories of estates, etc. … EVERYONE should own it if coins are involved in their activities. I highly recommend this book…"
– Lee Martin, Founder of the Numismatic Literary Guild

The first edition of this book, titled
The Rare Coin Estate Handbook, received many of
the comments and endorsements listed above, and
won the Robert Friedberg Award from the Professional
Numismatists Guild: Best Numismatic Book of the Year.
Now rewritten for all forms of art, jewelry
and collectibles, the 7th Edition of *The Collector's
Handbook* received the "Extraordinary Merit" award
from the Numismatic Literary Guild in 2013

.

Fr. 1202 $100 1882 Gold Certificate
PMG Very Fine 30
Sold for $750,000 | October 2022

Front Cover:

Rolex, Very Fine and Rare 14k Gold
Ref. 6241 "Paul Newman" Cosmograph
Daytona "John Player Special", Circa 1969
Sold for $804,500 | October 2018

1885 Trade Dollar
Finest of Five Examples Known
Sold for $3,960,000 | January 2019

Contents

1861 $20 Paquet
MS67 PCGS. CAC
Sold for $7,200,000 | August 2021

Foreword

:
:
:
:
:
:
:

WHY WE COLLECT THINGS

My friend John Jay Pittman did not start out a wealthy man. Slowly and with dedication, he assembled an incredible coin collection. He accomplished this through relentless study and at the cost of a significant portion of his limited income as a middle manager for Eastman Kodak, supplemented by his wife's income as a schoolteacher.

In 1954, John mortgaged the family house to travel to Egypt and bid on coins at the King Farouk Collection auction, and he demanded many more sacrifices of himself and his family over the decades. He passed away in 1996 with no apparent regrets, and his long-suffering family deservingly reaped the rewards of his efforts when the collection was sold at auction for more than $30 million.

But why did he do it?

On our website, HA.com, we auction many different types of collectibles; what started in 1976 as a numismatics business is now the largest auction house founded in America — with annual sales exceeding $1.45 billion in 2022 in categories ranging from meteorites to Hermès handbags. Most of our more than 1.75 million registered client/bidders collect in more than one area, which we can determine through online surveys, free catalog subscriptions, and multiple drawings for prizes throughout the year. Our clients pursue many different collecting areas, and for many different reasons.

One fervent collector of historical documents refers to his passion as "a genetic defect." The founding father of psychoanalysis Sigmund Freud, a renowned collector in his own right, thought that collecting was really about sex: "The core of paranoia is the detachment of the libido from objects," he wrote in 1908. "A reverse course is taken by the collector who directs his surplus libido into an inanimate object: a love of things." But more likely it's basic human instinct: a survival advantage amplified by eons of natural selection. Those of our ancient ancestors who managed to accumulate scarce objects may have been more likely to survive long enough to bear offspring—and people who owned shiny objects may have had an easier time attracting mates. Even today, wealth correlates with longer life expectancy; and could any form of wealth be more primal than scarce, tangible objects?

While the thrill of the hunt and a passion for objects — whether it's Lithuanian first-day covers or Alberto Vargas paintings — is what motivates and excites collectors, there are, alas, some housekeeping chores that must be tended to in order to assure that you derive the most benefit from your collection. Whether that means minimizing your tax burden, ensuring that your objects are safe from intruders, or maximizing your collection's value for your heirs, a little attention now can save you a massive headache later. It also will help you to get as much as you can out of the top 10 reasons Heritage Auctions' clients tell us that they collect (not in order):

1. Knowledge and learning

2. Relaxation and stress reduction

3. Personal pleasure

4. Social interaction with fellow collectors

5. Competitive challenge

6. Public recognition

7. Altruism (leaving a collection to a museum or non-profit organization)

8. The desire to control, possess and bring order to something

9. Nostalgia and/or a connection to history

10. Accumulation and diversification of wealth

Like Pittman, Robert Lesser is a true collector, but also a visionary with the ability to change his own course. He funded his later collections by assembling a fine collection of Disney memorabilia before it was popular, and later sold it for a seven-figure sum after the collecting world had come to appreciate it. Long before others discovered Disney memorabilia's now-obvious appeal, Lesser assembled preeminent collections of toy robots—museum exhibitions of his collection have attracted sell-out crowds with waiting lines stretching over city blocks—and pulp magazine cover paintings.

Many non-acquisitive pastimes provide similar levels of satisfaction, knowledge and recognition, along with the other benefits of collecting. But unlike home gardeners and tropical fish enthusiasts, serious collectors of rare objects will very often find that they have created substantial wealth—especially if they recognize this as one of the goals of their collections.

Whatever your motivation for collecting, this book will make you a more intelligent collector. Following the advice of our expert team of industry professionals, accountants, and lawyers will help you enjoy your collection more and ensure that your heirs can benefit from your legacy.

James L. Halperin
Co-Chairman, Heritage Auctions

Birger Sandzén (American, 1871-1954)
Lake at Sunset, Colorado, 1921
Oil on canvas
80 x 60 inches
Sold for $670,000 | May 2016
PROPERTY FROM A MIDWESTERN INSTITUTION

WORLD AUCTION RECORD FOR THE ARTIST

Acknowledgements

.
.
.
.
.
.

Writing a book is like forming a great collection: many people contribute in many different ways. While collecting, we build on the work of dealers, auction firms, friends old and new, and those dedicated authors whose reference books line our shelves. It is no different here. We offer many thanks to the following for their assistance during the preparation of this work:

Steve Ivy, Bob Korver, Burnett Marus, Steve Roach, Matthew S. Wilcox, Will Rossman, Richard Freeland, Noah Fleisher, Mark Van Winkle, Mark Masat, Brian Keagy, Michelle Castro, Taylor Strander, Deborah Daly, Steve Lansdale, Brett Flagg, Chris Britton, Jonathan Fehr, and Emily Murrah.

Henrietta Rae (British, 1859-1928)
Psyche before the throne of Venus, 1894
Oil on canvas
76-1/2 x 120 inches
Sold for $324,500 | May 2017
PROPERTY OF A TEXAS MUSEUM

Charlton Heston "Moses"
Signature Robe from
The Ten Commandments
(Paramount, 1956).
Sold for $447,000 | December 2022

Introduction

Collectors know the joy that comes from being surrounded by wonderful objects. The study of the pieces in our collections adds depth, color, and richness to our lives. We also know that a collection is intensely personal, and thus can be infrequently shared with others. You know your collection intimately. More than likely, your heirs do not.

Heritage's Appraisal Services team once encountered a collector who showed up at an appraisal fair with a meticulously kept book detailing every object she had in her collection: when she bought it, who she bought it from, what she paid for it and everything she knew about it.

Such meticulousness is rare. All too often, the chaos left behind by collectors leaves their descendants with a tax burden that could have been avoided, along with endless amounts of paperwork, legal fees, wrangling and other drama.

The principals at Heritage Auctions have written this book to provide information essential to collectors organizing their collections, advisors working with these collections and heirs who have inherited collections. Organizations that have received collections as donations also will benefit from this book.

1947 Jackie Robinson Game Worn Brooklyn Dodgers Rookie "Color Barrier" Jersey, MEARS A9 – Photo Matched with Family Provenance.
Sold for $2,050,000 | November 2017

PART ONE

Administering Your Collection

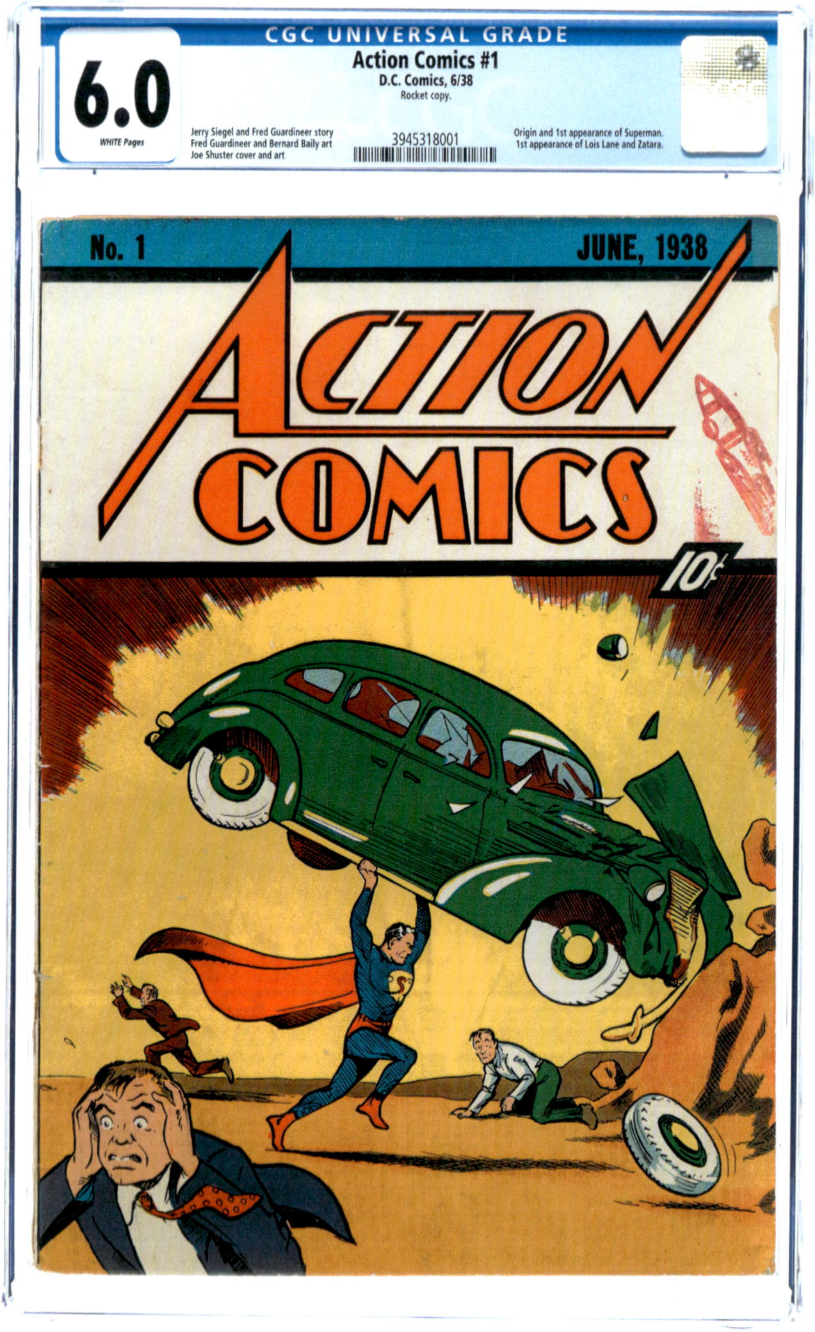

CGC UNIVERSAL GRADE

6.0

WHITE Pages

Action Comics #1
D.C. Comics, 6/38
Rocket copy.

Jerry Siegel and Fred Guardineer story
Fred Guardineer and Bernard Baily art
Joe Shuster cover and art

3945318001

Origin and 1st appearance of Superman.
1st appearance of Lois Lane and Zatara.

No. 1   **JUNE, 1938**

ACTION COMICS

10¢

Action Comics #1 Rocket Copy (DC, 1938)
CGC FN 6.0 White pages.
Sold for $3,180,000 | January 2022

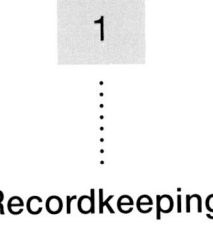

Recordkeeping

Mother: "This is the fertility vase of the Ndebele tribe.
Does that mean anything to you?"
Daughter: "No?"   – From the 2004 movie *Mean Girls*

We once appraised a home with six federal mahogany chests of drawers. The deceased's estate plan stipulated that a certain heir should receive "the good one." While the collector certainly understood which of the six was "the good one," he was not there to help—and the executor and attorney had no idea what he was talking about.

In another case involving a room full of paintings, the estate plan provided instructions for a certain painting: "the one with the banana." The heirs, executor and attorney all looked to us to determine which painting represented a banana. Unfortunately, it was impossible to find any resemblance in the group because all of the pieces were entirely abstract.

These situations sound like vaudeville skits, but both really happened— and they could have been avoided if the collections had been inventoried and numbered. Even when the terms of the will specify the exact location of an item in an effort to distinguish it from similar ones, it may not be enough. As collectors relocate, downsize, or simply rearrange their homes, the location of an item may change. Assigning a unique identification number does not change and therefore remains the only reliable method of inventorying items that we recommend.

Documenting what you own by writing it down by hand or in a printable listing is the most fundamental part of intelligent collections management. For historians and scholars, original handwritten inventories have proved to be invaluable tools with tasks as varied as accurately restoring a historic building, understanding a major battle or reconstructing a seminal art collection. The oldest known examples of writing in Europe are lists of commodities found in the storerooms of palaces in Ancient Greece. Modern technology has made the process easier than ever, and all collectors must understand the importance of proper documentation: It will be essential to your relationships with insurers, dealers, auction houses, the IRS and your heirs. Inputting and documenting each new acquisition as you proceed makes this process manageable.

The first question to answer: handwritten or digital? While it's possible to maintain meticulous paper records, our preference is that you use a computer program that is properly backed up in case of computer issues by a simple Excel spreadsheet, a Quicken list, a personal website, handwritten note cards, the MyCollection™ feature on the Heritage website or even some private software options like Collectify®. While doing anything at all will put you far ahead of most collectors, the more detailed, uniform and decipherable your inventory method is to the novice eye, the better. Your inventory system must be self-explanatory because you may not be there to explain it. Highly specialized jargon, abbreviations and personal notation codes should be avoided.

HA.com has a free feature called MyCollection™ which allows the collector to keep a private record. For coin and comic collectors, the feature is particularly useful because you will be able to quickly see market values for your pieces. HA.com/MyCollection

Different types of collectible property require different information fields, but a general checklist might appear as follows:

- **Object type**: What is it?

- **Title**: Does it have a known or descriptive title?

- **Maker**: Is the creator known?

- **Medium**: What's it made of?

- **Size**: Dimensions and/or weight?

- **Inscriptions**: Is anything written on it?

- **Signature**: Did the maker sign it? Where and how?

- **Subject**: Is there a representation on the item?

- **Date**: When was it made?

- **Manner of Acquisition**: How did you obtain it? (Auction, yard sale, etc.)

- **Cost/Date of Acquisition**: What did you pay for it? When did you buy it?

- **Location**: Where is the item? A safe deposit box, file cabinet, on loan to local museum? Specifics are important; if it's in a binder, say where the binder is located. For example, if a painting is in the living room above the sofa, note the location and the date the information was entered.

- **Provenance**: What is the item's history of ownership?

- **Special Notes**: Anything else you would want an heir to know about it? More information is always better. For example, has it been exhibited or published in a catalog?

- **Photographs**: Take a picture of each item in your collection.

- **File Folder**: Keep or scan copies of all relevant documentation: invoices, auction catalog entries, bills of lading, etc.

- **Inventory Number**: See next page.

Tiffany Studios Leaded Glass and Gilt Bronze
Drophead Dragonfly Table Lamp, circa 1910.
Sold for $275,000 | April 2022
Property from the Collection of Jeep & Carla Harned

The Art of Inventory Control: Tying it all Together

Even the most accurate inventory documentation can end up useless
if it is not "tied" to actual objects. Tying data to an object involves
giving each item a unique inventory number with which it is tagged or
marked, and then cross-referencing that tag with the written inventory
entry and a photograph.

A useful collection inventory number system should begin with the year
of acquisition, followed by an individual item number. For instance,
2016.001 would be reserved for the first piece acquired in the year
2016. This is the inventorying system used by museums, and with good
reason, since it is both predictable and easy to follow.

It is critical that the object, photograph, number tag and master inventory do not become separated. String tags and sticker labels often are used when safe to apply, and they can be removed easily; of course, this is easier with some objects than others. Museums generally look for a part of the object that is out of sight when on display — usually the bottom or back — and put a small strip of varnish down. After it dries, the ID number is written in ink, and when that dries, another coat of varnish is placed over the number. For paintings, only the back stretchers or frames should be marked with the work's unique ID number. Each type of property presents its own numbering challenges. Often, the only solution is to tag the box or plastic sleeve in which an object is stored, but this is not ideal since boxes and sleeves can be switched. Today, bar code technology, microchips and even radioactive isotope staining have enhanced our tagging options. Do your research to see what's out there and what's best for your particular collection. Ask dealers who specialize in the category, and seek out the advice of societies that serve collectors. Find out what the best practices are for each category you collect. A key principle is that a tagging or numbering system should never damage an item.

When photographing an object, write its unique ID number on a piece of paper and place it in the picture field so that the photograph actually displays the object and the number. That way, any loose photograph can be easily identified. Most large collections contain near-identical or duplicate items that, to the untrained eye, may appear indistinguishable from one another, even though values can vary widely. Many coin collections have been spent by heirs who were unaware that the coins had value to collectors, and this fate could be avoided with proper identification.

You will thank yourself in the long run, as will everyone involved!

Finally, maintain a second copy of your complete inventory, including photographs, in a different location from the collection itself. Safe deposit boxes in banks are recommended, and it also is a good idea to have an electronic copy stored on a backup disc and/or online.

When you sell or otherwise remove an item from your collection, make certain that it is noted clearly in your inventory—unless, of course, you despise your heirs and wish to send them on a decades-long hunt for a valuable object you sold 20 years ago.

Norman Rockwell (American, 1894-1978) *Home for Thanksgiving, The Saturday Evening Post cover,* November 24, 1945
Sold for $4,305,000 | November 2021
Property from the E.M. Connor Post #193 American Legion, Winchendon, Massachusetts, Being Sold To Benefit Operational and Building Funds

Caring For Your Collection

"He that thinks he can afford to be negligent is not far from being poor." – Samuel Johnson

"Never neglect details." – Colin Powell

After being created, all objects age; they act and react over time in accordance with their physical and chemical properties, combined with the environment in which they're stored. Metals mineralize naturally. Paper collectibles are photo-chemically changed when exposed to the light necessary for us to enjoy them. Soft fabrics become brittle and hard substances become pliable. While some changes may take centuries, others take only minutes — and the goal of the collector, like that of the museum conservator or a Hollywood actor, should be to minimize damage and slow the aging process.

Human contact is the leading culprit of wear and deterioration. Use of an object, whether it is a circulated coin or toy train, takes a toll. For many items, use reduces value, but in others, it increases it. A baseball glove worn out by 10 years of continued use by Ted Williams has greater value because of its history, regardless of the physical condition that results from aging. For baseball cards, part of the value comes from their ability to withstand the long odds of survival: cards cut from recently discovered sheets are seen as second-class citizens. Each category of collectible has its own standard that governs the effects of original use on value. Once an object has left its original environment and becomes a cultural collectible, the new owners must endeavor to preserve its condition.

Human touch can harm objects physically and chemically through the acids in perspiration. After that, sunlight and moisture are the two greatest destroyers of most collections. Another serious threat is contact with reactive materials such as a cleansing or sealing agent.

Human Contact

Avoiding direct contact with objects, if possible, is best.

- Coins can be placed in sealed inert capsules, which protect them from both physical and chemical harm. If outside a capsule, a coin should only be grasped by its edge, avoiding contact with its two sides. Paintings should be framed using archival materials; prints should be glazed, then framed. Grasp only the frames when examining. Comics should be placed in Mylar sleeves or encapsulated by Certified Guaranty Company (CGC).

- White cotton gloves should be worn when handling anything directly, but be aware that your grip may be affected by wearing gloves. When examining a valuable ceramic lidded jar, place one hand on the lid and the other under the base, so that the lid does not fall off while being moved. Statues in any medium should never be grasped by their extending parts (for instance, the arms or legs of figural works).

Sunlight and Artificial Light

If you have ever noticed a rich dark mahogany table bleached off-white and cracked because of its location near a window, or a once-vibrant watercolor painting that has faded dramatically, you have witnessed the powerful effect of light on objects. Prolonged exposure to ultraviolet light may destroy valuable furniture, paintings, photographs, books and textiles.

If you wish to keep your collections in plain view, certain steps should be taken to minimize light damage:

- Purchase windows that filter UV light.

- Place UV filter sleeves over fluorescent lighting.

- Glaze framed items with UV filtering acrylic, not glass (not appropriate for all media).

- Hang curtains and blinds to filter sunlight.

- Never position a light-sensitive object in direct sunlight.

- Keep sensitive works covered with protective cloth; remove only when viewing.

1909 T206 Sweet Caporal
Honus Wagner
(The Garagiola Wagner)
SGC Authentic.
Sold for $2,520,000
February 2021

SGC

1909 SWEET CAPORAL
T206 HONUS WAGNER
(THE GARAGIOLA WAGNER)

A ⬡

6011014

PITTSBURG

WAGNER, PITTSBURG

IN CONGRESS,

JULY 4, 1776.

A DECLARATION

BY THE

REPRESENTATIVES

OF THE

UNITED STATES OF AMERICA,

IN GENERAL CONGRESS ASSEMBLED.

WHEN in the course of human events, it becomes necessary for one people to dissolve the political bands which have connected them with another, and to assume among the powers of the earth, the separate and equal station to which the laws of nature and of nature's God entitle them, a decent respect to the opinions of mankind requires that they should declare the causes which impel them to the separation.

We hold these truths to be self-evident, that all men are created equal, that they are endowed by their Creator with certain unalienable rights, that among these are life, liberty, and the pursuit of happiness. That to secure these rights, governments are instituted among men, deriving their just powers from the consent of the governed, that whenever any form of government becomes destructive of these ends, it is the right of the people to alter or to abolish it, and to institute new government, laying its foundation on such principles, and organizing its powers in such form, as to them shall seem most likely to effect their safety and happiness. Prudence, indeed, will dictate that governments long established should not be changed for light and transient causes; and accordingly all experience hath shewn, that mankind are more disposed to suffer, while evils are sufferable, than to right themselves by abolishing the forms to which they are accustomed. But when a long train of abuses and usurpations, pursuing invariably the same object, evinces a design to reduce them under absolute despotism, it is their right, it is their duty, to throw off such government, and to provide new guards for their future security. Such has been the patient sufferance of these Colonies; and such is now the necessity which constrains them to alter their former systems of government. The history of the present King of Great-Britain is a history of repeated injuries and usurpations, all having in direct object the establishment of an absolute tyranny over these States. To prove this, let facts be submitted to a candid world.

He has refused his assent to laws, the most wholesome and necessary for the public good.

He has forbidden his Governors to pass laws of immediate and pressing importance, unless suspended in their operation until his assent should be obtained; and when so suspended, he has utterly neglected to attend them.

He has refused to pass other laws for the accommodation of large districts of people, unless those people would relinquish the right of representation in the legislature, a right inestimable to them, and formidable to Tyrants only.

He has called together legislative bodies at places unusual, uncomfortable, and distant from the depository of their public records, for the sole purpose of fatiguing them into compliance with his measures.

He has dissolved representative houses repeatedly, for opposing with manly firmness his invasions on the rights of the people.

He has refused for a long time, after such dissolutions, to cause others to be elected; whereby the legislative powers, incapable of annihilation, have returned to the people at large for their exercise; the state remaining in the mean time exposed to all the dangers of invasion from without, and convulsions within.

He has endeavoured to prevent the population of these States; for that purpose obstructing the laws for naturalization of foreigners; refusing to pass others to encourage their migrations hither, and raising the conditions of new appropriations of lands.

He has obstructed the administration of justice, by refusing his assent to laws for establishing judiciary powers.

He has made Judges dependent on his will alone, for the tenure of their offices, and the amount and payment of their salaries.

He has erected a multitude of new offices, and sent hither swarms of officers to harrass our people, and eat out their substance.

He has kept among us, in times of peace, standing armies, without the consent of our Legislatures.

He has affected to render the military independent of and superior to the civil power.

He has combined with others to subject us to a jurisdiction foreign to our constitution and unacknowledged by our laws; giving his assent to their acts of pretended legislation:

For quartering large bodies of armed troops among us:

For protecting them, by a mock trial, from punishment for any murders which they should commit on the inhabitants of these States:

For cutting off our trade with all parts of the world:

For imposing taxes on us without our consent:

For depriving us, in many cases, of the benefits of trial by jury:

For transporting us beyond seas to be tried for pretended offences:

For abolishing the free system of English laws in a neighboring province, establishing therein an arbitrary government, and enlarging its boundaries, so as to render it at once an example and fit instrument for introducing the same absolute rule into these Colonies:

For taking away our Charters, abolishing our most valuable laws, and altering fundamentally the forms of our governments:

For suspending our own Legislatures, and declaring themselves invested with power to legislate for us in all cases whatsoever.

He has abdicated government here, by declaring us out of his protection and waging war against us.

He has plundered our seas, ravaged our coasts, burnt our towns, and destroyed the lives of our people.

He is at this time, transporting large armies of foreign mercenaries to compleat the works of death, desolation and tyranny, already begun with circumstances of cruelty and perfidy scarcely paralleled in the most barbarous ages, and totally unworthy the head of a civilized nation.

He has constrained our fellow citizens taken captive on the high seas to bear arms against their country, to become the executioners of their friends and brethren, or to fall themselves by their hands.

He has excited domestic insurrections amongst us, and has endeavored to bring on the inhabitants of our frontiers, the merciless Indian savages, whose known rule of warfare, is an undistinguished destruction of all ages, sexes, and conditions.

In every stage of these oppressions we have petitioned for redress, in the most humble terms: Our repeated petitions have been answered only by repeated injury. A Prince, whose character is thus marked by every act which may define a Tyrant, is unfit to be the Ruler of a free People.

Nor have we been wanting in attention to our British brethren. We have warned them from time to time of attempts by their legislature to extend an unwarrantable jurisdiction over us. We have reminded them of the circumstances of our emigration and settlement here. We have appealed to their native justice and magnanimity, and we have conjured them by the ties of our common kindred to disavow these usurpations, which would inevitably interrupt our connections and correspondence. They too have been deaf to the voice of justice and of consanguinity. We must, therefore, acquiesce in the necessity which denounces our separation, and hold them, as we hold the rest of mankind, enemies in war; in peace, friends.

We, therefore, the Representatives of the UNITED STATES OF AMERICA, in GENERAL CONGRESS assembled, appealing to the supreme Judge of the world for the rectitude of our intentions, do in the name and by the authority of the good People of these Colonies, solemnly publish and declare, That these United Colonies are, and of right ought to be, FREE AND INDEPENDENT STATES; that they are absolved from all allegiance to the British Crown, and that all political connection between them and the State of Great-Britain, is, and ought to be totally dissolved; and that as FREE AND INDEPENDENT STATES, they have full power to levy war, conclude peace, contract alliances, establish commerce, and to do all other acts and things which INDEPENDENT STATES may of right do. And for the support of this Declaration, with a firm reliance on the protection of Divine Providence, we mutually pledge to each other our lives, our fortunes, and our sacred honor.

Signed by ORDER *and in* BEHALF *of the* CONGRESS,

JOHN HANCOCK, PRESIDENT.

ATTEST,

CHARLES THOMPSON, Secretary.

Water and Moisture

"For my birthday I got a humidifier and a dehumidifier. I put them in the same room and let them fight it out." – Steven Wright

Most water damage is caused not by rain, burst pipes or floods, but by humidity. Organic materials deteriorate in humid conditions; mold and mildew can grow, and metals mineralize at a faster rate.

The recommended relative humidity (RH) for your collections should be determined (check with a dealer or society that specializes in your field), after which you need to take the necessary steps to protect your collections from air conditioning, humidifying and dehumidifying. It is important to avoid large fluctuations in RH and temperature, as these fluctuations may cause serious stress to any object. Here are the recommended storage conditions for a few of our most popular categories:

- Books: 68°F to 72°F, with 40 to 50 percent relative humidity.
- Comic Books: 50°F to 65°F — and it's important to keep the temperature consistent. 40 to 60 percent relative humidity is recommended.
- Coins (and other metals): The biggest concern here is relative humidity. Below 30 percent is ideal.
- Historic Paper: The Preservation Directorate at The Library of Congress says it stores documents at 50°F with relative humidity of 50 percent.
- Paintings: 68°F is recommended, with relatively humidity at around 50 percent.
- Stamps: 65°F and 50 percent relative humidity is the recommendation from *Linn's Stamp News*.

Reactive Materials

It is not unusual to find 19th-century prints on pulp paper in their original frames, with acid-rich mats fixed with glued tape, backed by thin planks of pine and secured with iron-alloy nails. We since have learned a great deal about reactive chemistry and understand that the old practices are truly bad.

The acid in the mat leaks out to the print, causing discoloration or mat burn. Other acids in the adhesive tape do the same. The wood

Retro Raymond Yard Citrine,
Gold Jewelry Suite
Sold for $250,000 | May 2022
Property from the Cary M. Maguire Estate, Dallas, Texas

This suite was
commissioned by Joan
Crawford from famed
jeweler Raymond Yard. After
receiving it, she wore it in
the film *Where Ladies Meet*
(1941) and in a print ad for
Royal Crown Cola.

backer and frame, which are designed to protect the print, are full of acetic acid, formic acid, formaldehyde and other chemicals that can do serious damage. Finally, the iron nails reacting to the wood and moist air corrode quickly, harming anything in close proximity.

Today, even our urban, industrialized air contains sulfur dioxide and nitrogen dioxide that can create an acidic environment in the presence of elevated relative humidity.

It is imperative that collectors learn what conditions will affect their particular collections. Outdoor marble statuary will not be harmed greatly by sunlight or termites, but acid rain will do the job quickly unless a protective wax is applied regularly. Some modern art is created with materials that are meant to change over time, and that change is part of the artist's intention. Every category of art, antiques and collectibles has its own preservation requirements.

Educate Yourself

Don't assume the frames, wrappers, backboards, plastic sleeves or other materials that house your artworks or collectibles at the time of purchase are the safest ones available for the continued health of your acquisitions. The fact that many collectibles have appreciated in value over time means that a costlier means of preservation may be more justified today than when an item originally was sold.

Caring for your collection properly requires learning the safest and most updated methods available for viewing, displaying and storing items. Each object will have unique issues relevant to its own material, form and condition.

Museum and conservation information is readily available in books and online. A good reference is *Conservation Concerns: A Guide for Collectors and Curators*, edited by Konstanze Bachman. For more advice on issues surrounding storage and preservation, check with reputable dealers, auctioneers, and collectors' societies.

Star Power Stallone
The Auction

Most collectors get to a point at which they decide to downsize, and this includes celebrities. Celebrity connections have the ability to increase the value of otherwise ordinary items. Sylvester Stallone called Heritage Auctions when he decided to sell items from his personal collection that spanned his long career in Hollywood.

Stallone wanted to be part of the sales process and stayed through several hours of the first day's bidding, interacting with fans and posing for pictures. "The memorabilia I have has been used and been a part of my life for — kind of hard to admit this— well over 40 years," Stallone said. "It has been in my possession and I have fond memories attached to just about every object. There comes a point, though, when I think that I've used these objects enough and have created enough memories that I can let them go."

Heritage's sale, titled "Stallone – The Auction" took place Dec. 18-20, 2015, and included dozens of his most iconic costumes, props and personal items. Some of the items included the leather jacket that Stallone wore as a costume in the first *Rocky* movie in 1976, which doubled its estimate when it sold for $149,000. On the jacket, Stallone reminisced, "I remember when I bought this jacket. It was obviously quite a few years before I ever even thought about *Rocky*, before *Rocky* was even an idea. This is what I would wear in my everyday life, and when the time came to do the movie, we didn't have a budget where we could afford an original wardrobe so I thought, 'Why don't I just wear the things that I think *Rocky* would wear, clothes from my real life?' So, I went in my closet, pulled out this jacket. It's one of those unique times where life imitates art, art imitates reality. This jacket was used in several of the films and it really established Rocky as kind of mythical, dark knight character. You knew something special was going to happen with this individual because he just looked different — and this black leather jacket set the tone for the rest of the series."

A used leather jacket that would be worth perhaps $30 in a secondhand store, described in the auction catalog as a "Small collar, five button front closure, two front pockets, two distinct pleats at shoulders, black faux fur zip-out lining," became worth nearly $150,000 due to its connection to a great actor and a classic film. Stallone helped Heritage in crafting the lot descriptions, adding priceless first-hand anecdotes that likely encouraged the robust bidding. In total, 13 bidders competed for the lot, with the winning bid being placed online at HA Live.

The Stallone sale realized more than $3 million. Beyond sharing his personal history with thousands of fans, Stallone donated a portion of the proceeds to various charities that assist military veterans and wounded servicemen and servicewomen as well as The Motion Picture and TV Country House and Hospital.

A Sylvester Stallone
Personal Black Leather
Jacket from "Rocky."
Sold for $149,000 | December 2015

The Estate Gift of
Mary Anne Sammons Cree

Dallas, Texas native Mary Anne Sammons Cree quietly and powerfully supported many passions during her lifetime, often focusing on opportunities for her community to experience the wonder of the arts and the natural world. So generous was Cree that even after her passing, she continued to give back to her beloved hometown.

In September 2022, Heritage Auctions offered more than 125 pieces from Cree's extraordinary jewelry collection as the centerpiece of our Fall Fine Jewelry Signature® Auction. Proceeds from the sale of Cree's jewelry supported The Rosine Fund of Communities Foundation of Texas, so named for Mary Anne's mother, from whom she inherited her spirit of giving.

"As a Dallas-based auction house, it was kismet for Heritage Auctions to partner with Communities Foundation of Texas to present Mary Anne's stunning jewelry collection to collectors worldwide," says Michelle Castro, Vice President of Trusts & Estates.

Fancy Intense Yellow Diamond Ring
Sold for $591,000

David Webb Jewelry Suite
Sold for $47,500

Fancy Yellow Diamond Earrings
Sold for $225,000

1787 DBLN New York-Style Brasher
Doubloon, EB on Wing,
MS65★ NGC. CAC. W-5840.
Sold for $9,360,000 | January 2021

························

3

Safeguarding Your Collection

"If you didn't have so much stuff, you wouldn't need a house. You could just walk around all the time. A house is just a pile of stuff with a cover on it." – George Carlin

Crimes against property are on the rise, and the reasons that fine art, antiques and collectibles are great investments are the same reasons they're great targets for thieves. The current arrest and conviction rate is abysmal, and the odds of recovering stolen goods are even lower. With budget constraints forcing law enforcement to deprioritize property crimes, the outlook for a reversal in that trend is not good. The only solution is to do what you can to protect your collection against criminals — and make sure that it is properly insured in the event that you are the victim of a crime (or natural disaster).

Security vs. Access

Most collectors want their treasures close at hand to study and enjoy — even though that is a suboptimal loss prevention strategy. To alleviate this, write your own personal security plan and include these elements:

- Security
  Your collection is at risk from theft, fire, water damage and other natural disasters. If you are going to have objects of substantial value at your residence, you should consider several proactive measures to protect them.

- Monitored Security System
  A monitored system is at the core of any security plan. This includes both theft and fire alarms that are monitored externally and immediately reported directly to police and fire departments when triggered. Hardware can be installed for a few hundred to a few thousand dollars, and monitoring involves a monthly expense,

currently around $25 to $75. A monitored security system sends most burglars looking for easier targets and puts the more daring ones on the clock. Once the system perimeter is breached, the burglar has only the response time to grab what he can and attempt an escape. This might seem like a pain and a substantial investment, but there are advantages. According to the Insurance Information Institute, the average homeowner's insurance discount provided based on the presence of a monitored security system is between 15 and 20 percent; according to the Electronic Security Association, the average loss on a home with a system is $3,266, compared with $5,343 for an unprotected home. But wait! There's more! You'll also be protecting your neighborhood as a whole: A 2009 study out of the School of Criminal Justice at Rutgers University found that the higher the percentage of homes in a neighborhood that have security systems, the fewer break-ins occur in that neighborhood — providing a benefit even to residents who don't have a security system.

- Home Safe
A safe can be an excellent way to protect valuables and important documents from theft or damage, but choosing one that meets your needs can be challenging. Safes are rated on their burglary and fire resistance. Some safes offer significant protection against burglary but offer no fire protection. Others may be able to withstand heat for hours but are not rated against attacks from power tools.

The cost of a safe is primarily a function of its protection ratings and size. The larger a safe is and the more protection it offers, the more expensive it will be. Additionally, insurance companies may have specific requirements for a home safe. A reputable safe dealer should be able to help you select a model that meets your budget, protection needs, physical space, and any applicable insurance requirements.

- Deterrent Practices
There are other actions that reduce the risk of a successful burglary. Always leave the impression that someone is at home. This can be accomplished in part by remembering to have your paper and mail held while you are out of town and by placing one or more of your lights on timers. "Beware of Dog" signs are helpful in warding off potential burglars and also can reduce your Halloween expenditures.

**Abraham Lincoln: Outstanding
Signed Carte-de-Visite.**
Sold for $175,000 | September 2016

- Camouflaging Valuables

  Most people are predictable, and experienced burglars know all the "good" hiding places. Typically, most people keep their valuables in the master bedroom and home office. Guess where burglars go first? So, try to avoid these typical hiding spots and leave decoys. One gentleman we know has numerous coin albums (filled with pocket change) in plain sight on the bookshelves. Another has an old safe that is heavy but moveable. It resides in the corner of his home office and contains absolutely nothing. Its predecessor was removed in a burglary during which the thief left behind several thousand dollars' worth of electronics because he thought the safe was the jackpot. He now has a monitored security system and modern wall safe, but still keeps a decoy as a reminder of the importance of security and the burglar who was the recipient of nothing but an empty box (and perhaps a hernia). If you don't own a safe, small valuables are best hidden in a false outlet with an object plugged into it. A collection of small items should be spread over several non-obvious locations.

Off-Site Storage & Transport

The primary off-site storage option is a safe deposit box at either a bank or private vault. If you can find a location close to home or work, the inconvenience factor can be minimized. Sites with weekend access offer a major advantage. Remember that while safe deposit boxes offer secure storage, vigilance is still important. Here are a few storage and security guidelines you need to remember and follow:

- Rent a box that is large enough to hold everything easily.

- Use a desiccant such as silica gel to remove any moisture, and change it regularly.

- Never forget that your greatest security danger is in transporting the collectibles to and from the box. Use a nondescript container to hold them, and try not to carry too much weight at once.

- Have someone drive you to the location, or, if you must drive yourself, park as close to the entrance as possible to minimize your time on the street with the valuables.

- Avoid establishing a pattern in picking up or dropping off your collection.

- Be aware of your surroundings when transporting your collectibles. Check your rearview mirror frequently, and if you believe you're being followed, do not drive directly to your destination. Make several detours that do not follow any logical traffic pattern and see if you are able to lose the suspect vehicle. Know the location of the closest police station, and if you can't lose your stalker, drive there directly. We know this sounds a little like a made-for-TV movie, but it's important.

- Carry a cell phone with you when transporting valuables. A frightening robbery technique is to rear-end a vehicle and then rob the driver when he or she exits to assess the damage and exchange insurance information. You will have to use your judgment in this situation, but if you are carrying valuables and are rear-ended, you should remain in the car and call 911. Don't hesitate to tell the operator that you are carrying valuables and are concerned about the possibility of robbery. If you really believe that it is a setup, don't stop — call 911 and explain the situation while driving to the police station.

With their steady flow of people, noise and confusion, airports have also become a favorite hub for thieves. The usual method is the snatch-and-grab; the thief targets someone who appears distracted, grabs the briefcase or bag and melts into the crowd.

A variation is the use of teams of criminals located where baggage is being unloaded at the curb. A few of the thieves distract the victim while others grab the bags, after which all of them make their escape in a waiting vehicle.

Hermès Extraordinary 30cm Matte White Himalayan Niloticus Crocodile Birkin Bag with Palladium Hardware.
Sold for $140,000 | September 2021

Your only protection is constant vigilance. You should always either have a grip or your foot on any case containing valuables.

Some people carry a loud whistle when transporting valuables. If someone attempts to grab a bag and you start blowing the whistle, the thief is put on the defensive. Everyone else in the area is confused or startled by the noise and the thief loses the camouflage of the crowd.

Shipping

First and foremost, do not attach anything to the outside of the package that would hint at its contents. When Ty Inc., the company behind Beanie Babies, realized that boxes were being lost during shipping in huge quantities at the height of that mania, it made a simple change by removing its logo from the boxes. Consequently, theft shrank dramatically. If a package contains any identifying words, such as "coins," in the mailing address or on the outer wrapping, it makes the contents of that package more appealing to thieves.

Pack the items securely so that they do not rattle. Loose spaces (such as in tubes) should be filled. Styrofoam "peanuts" are good for this purpose. Make sure that your shipping box is strong enough for the included weight, then bind it with strapping tape. If you are using Registered Mail (the preferred method for most collectors to ship small packages containing valuable items), the Post Office has a requirement that all access seams be sealed with an approved paper tape. Including the word "fragile" in large letters on the package may prevent rough handling by carriers.

Method of shipment involves a decision that weighs value, risk and cost. USPS First Class or Priority Mail with insurance is the most cost-effective method for packages up to $500 in value. The rate of loss has dropped considerably over the last decade, making this a reasonable option for inexpensive items that can be replaced. Above the $500 value, Registered Mail with Postal Insurance is both cost-effective and extremely safe. The one caveat is that the insurance maximum for registered mail is $50,000. The Post Office requires you to indicate if the contents exceed that amount but it will not pay more than $50,000 on a claim. If the value exceeds that amount, you will need to send multiple packages or obtain supplemental private insurance.

FedEx, UPS and other private shippers have become popular in recent years, offering fast, guaranteed delivery with a high success rate. They also offer some insurance options, but rare coins and certain other collectibles are specifically excluded. You will need to obtain private insurance coverage if you use one of these shippers, or you may request that the other party insures the shipment if there is sufficient coverage available and a shipper account.

Insurance

No matter how many security measures you employ to protect your collection, you will also need to acquire suitable insurance to protect yourself. This can be a complicated area, as insurance companies write policies in a language all their own. As a collector, you need to be especially mindful of homeowner's insurance because you likely will require a policy that differs from a standard one.

A Tiffany & Co. Partial Gilt Silver Punch Bowl and Ladle Driving Trophy, New York, 1881
Sold for $118,750 | November 2020
American Presentation and Trophy Silver from the Collection of J.D. Parks

Coins Stored in Fake Plumbing, ...
Nearly Century-Old Safe Box

Coins hidden in fake plumbing and stored in a bank box that likely hadn't been opened in nearly a century were two of the tales Heritage Auctions President Greg Rohan told collectors attending his presentation on "Major Collections We've Auctioned – The Back Story" at the Central States convention.

After Jules Reiver, noted collector, researcher and writer, died in 2004 at 87, his family contracted with another dealer to sell his collection. Rohan said, "We were brought in. I went out to their house. It was a very modest house. I had been there before, and I remembered that Jules had to go under the kitchen sink to get coins out. He had them in fake pipes under the sink. So we got the coins that were at the house and went to the bank and got the coins that were at the bank."

Reiver's wife, Iona, who died in 2017 at 97, said her husband had always said his collection was worth $1 million. Heritage estimated it would bring $6 million to $7 million, a figure, Rohan said, he thought the family took with a grain of salt. The collection sold for more than $8 million. After the collection was sold, Rohan said Mrs. Reiver told him, "I feel just like the Beverly Hillbillies."

In 2015, Rohan said, Heritage was contacted by an art auction house about a coin collection that had been put together between 1850 and 1930 by the Rev. James G .K. McClure, pastor of First Presbyterian Church in Lake Forest, Ill., for 25 years. The coins, housed in custom cases, had sat largely untouched in a bank safe deposit box since McClure's death in 1932. "Boy, did that get my attention," Rohan said. "To see the coins that had been untouched since that time was one of the most extraordinary experiences."

The collection was notable for its depth, state of preservation and the way it was accumulated. Rohan said, "Rev. McClure got coins at a face value at the bank. There were a few times where there were coins that were harder to get, proof coins that he got as gifts from parishioners. He paid maybe a few dollars for some.

"Seeing his Walking Liberty halves, all of which he got at the bank at the time of circulation – the 1921, '21-D, '21-S. These coins were of unbelievable quality, unbelievable. ... I would look at rows of coins that were taken out of circulation that were worth just a few dollars each and then come to one that was worth a hundred thousand dollars."

He said a Chicago-area coin dealer had offered the family $840,000 for the collection. "Being intelligent and prudent people, they decided to get another opinion," he said. "Our estimate was $3 million to 3.5 million." The collection sold for $4.5 million at auction in 2016.

Heritage Auctions President Greg Rohan addresses bidders on Platinum Night.

The Gene Gardner collection, another collection Heritage handled, sold for $52.8 million in four sales in 2014 and 2015.

Rohan, who developed a personal friendship with Gardner before his death in 2016 at age 80, said Eugene Herr Gardner Sr. was born to a life of wealth and privilege. He had the wherewithal to build a notable collection while still in college in the 1960s, but his hobby didn't sit well with his family.

Rohan said, Gardner's "father was very upset with him for spending a few hundred thousand dollars in the 1960s on coins and thought it was a complete folly and a waste of money and that his son has lost his mind. So Gene sold the collection after he graduated from college and ... it brought $700,000.

"I think there was some 'I told you so's' around the dinner table. I don't think Gene's father ever questioned his business acumen ever again. He turned out to be one of the great investors of our time."

Gardner founded investment advisor Gardner Russo & Gardner, which, Rohan said, had more than $10 billion under management.

Gardner was diagnosed with multiple myeloma in 2010 and given a short time to live. At his wife's request, preparations for the first auction were speeded up so Gardner could witness the sale of some of his most-prized coins. However, he lived to see the entire collection sold, dying a few months after the last sale and six years after diagnosis.

This article was originally published in the Summer 2019 issue of the Central States Numismatic Society's journal, The Centinel, www.centralstatesnumismaticsociety.org. Reprinted with permission.

As someone seeking protection, you need to understand that contract language generally favors the insurance company, and you need to know exactly what coverage you are — and are not — receiving. That means asking questions and reading every word of every document in every policy you sign. In the case of coins, you need to be particularly certain of what coverage applies when the coins are at home, in a safe-deposit box or in transit, as well as any additional security requirements for each circumstance. Some things to keep in mind:

• Most homeowner's policies DO NOT insure your coin or jewelry collection beyond $1,000 (combined with all other items defined as a "valuable"). Most insurance companies will offer a rider for more specific coverage, but since it's not their standard business, they

Auguste Rodin (French, 1840-1917)
Éternel printemps, deuxième état, première reduction, 1899-1901
Bronze with brown-black patina
25-7/8 x 33-1/4 x 15-3/4 inches
Sold for $762,500 | December 2018

typically are not very flexible. You will be required to provide a fixed inventory, and modifying the coverage whenever you buy or sell items from your collection will likely require a major paperwork effort.

- Some insurance companies require an "appraisal for insurance." If you choose a company that has this requirement, guidance is available later in this book. In this specialized field, the best option often comes from a company that is familiar with the needs of collectors. We have listed several companies in Appendix B.

- In the case of collectibles other than coins, you may want to ask a dealer to recommend a knowledgeable insurance company. Not all insurance companies possess the expertise or coverage options that collectors require. While premiums vary, price is not the only consideration. Find an agent and a company with a good reputation and expertise in the field of collectibles. You may have to pay a little more, but it will be well worth the price if you ever have to submit a significant claim.

- One final note about security: You need to be careful about discussing your collection (and especially where you keep it) with others. Enjoy your collection, but stay vigilant. A little paranoia could save you hundreds of thousands of dollars.

TIPS FOR HEIRS: This chapter contains advice that may be the most important you will read. Seasoned collectors are generally very security-conscious, but those who have come into possession of a collection only recently must immediately understand the risks and responsibilities that come with this unfamiliar asset. If it's small enough, take the collection to a safe deposit box immediately. Until you have it safely transferred into a bank vault, do not discuss it with others. With larger objects, you may want to consult with an insurance agent about the best method to safeguard them until they have found their next home.

PART TWO

Estate Planning For Your Collection

1794 $1 B-1, BB-1, R.4,
MS66+ PCGS. CAC
Sold for $6,600,000 | August 2021
Bob R. Simpson Collection

4

All in the Family

Celebrities are just like us. Given their wealth, notoriety, and teams of advisors, we expect celebrities to have formal estate plans in place. Historically, it turns out that celebrities have more in common with "us" and often do not have the appropriate documentation and directives in place that will provide for their loved ones and secure their legacy once they are gone. Jimi Hendrix died in 1970, and his estate was subsequently the subject of 30 years of litigation — a very un-rock 'n' roll epilogue to an incredible career. Queen of Soul, Aretha Franklin's estate was involved in a long legal dispute over the singer's two handwritten wills, one in a locked cabinet and the other found in the couch. Neither document was prepared by a lawyer or listed witnesses, and both documents divided the singer's assets differently. Ultimately, a jury in Michigan probate court ruled that the handwritten document found in the couch represented the singer's true last wishes. Picasso was revered as a business genius during his lifetime, but when he died in 1973 without a proper will, his many heirs were thrust into chaos. It took six years and a reported $30 million in expenses to divide up his estate. More recently, musician Prince passed away in 2016 without a will, leaving a sizeable estate hanging in limbo. Prince's estate finally settled in 2022 after a six-year court battle.

One recent survey found that over half of Americans with children do not have a current estate plan. Most people try to avoid contemplating their own demise, and many collectors are equally reluctant to consider the sale of their treasures. As Woody Allen once told his physician, "Doctor, I'm not afraid of dying, I just don't want to be there when it happens."

Heritage Auctions' Trusts & Estates team assists professional advisors, executors, fiduciaries, and beneficiaries with confidential and comprehensive auction and formal appraisal services tailored to the unique needs of the estate or collection. We recognize that each client and appraisal project differs and often involves multi-category collections and residences. Our Trusts & Estates specialists offer complimentary walk-through services and bring together decades of experience appraising property in over fifty collecting categories. Beyond providing auction estimates for disposition purposes, our team assists with providing cost estimates for appraisal projects for charitable donations, gift taxes, loan collateral, and financial planning. Heritage Auctions Appraisals Services, Inc. prepares appraisals for one item or large, multi-category collections.

Headquartered in Dallas, Texas, and with offices in New York, Chicago, Beverly Hills and Palm Beach, Heritage is well-positioned to work with families and their advisors, providing creative solutions for estate planning with collectibles. We understand this process can be overwhelming and emotional; our goal at Heritage is to ensure a transparent and enjoyable legacy- planning experience for you and your family.

Involve Your Family

Many collectors keep their families in the dark regarding scale and nature of their collecting; there are many reasons for this, but consider taking a longer view. Have you thought about the effect that your sudden death or incapacitation might have on your collection? What would you expect from your heirs? What should be done with your collection? Should it be sold? Distributed among family members? Some combination? What will remain after taxes?

One call from a surviving spouse took us to a house where we found a dining room table covered with boxed world coins that were stacked three feet high. From a distance, it was one of the most impressive collections that we ever had inspected: all matching coin boxes, each neatly labeled with its country of origin. The surviving spouse told us that her husband had been a serious collector for more than three decades, visiting his local coin shop nearly every Saturday. He then came home and meticulously prepared his purchases, spending hour upon happy hour at the table in his little study.

We opened the first box and couldn't help but notice the neat, orderly presentation: cardboard 2x2 coin holders, neatly stapled, with crisp printing of country name, year of issue, Yeoman number, date of purchase and amount paid. We also couldn't help notice that 90 percent of the coins had been purchased for less than 50 cents and the balance for less than $1 each. The collection contained box after box of post-1940 minors — all impeccably presented and all essentially worthless.

We asked the surviving spouse if she had any idea of the value of the collection. She replied that she knew rare coins were valuable, and

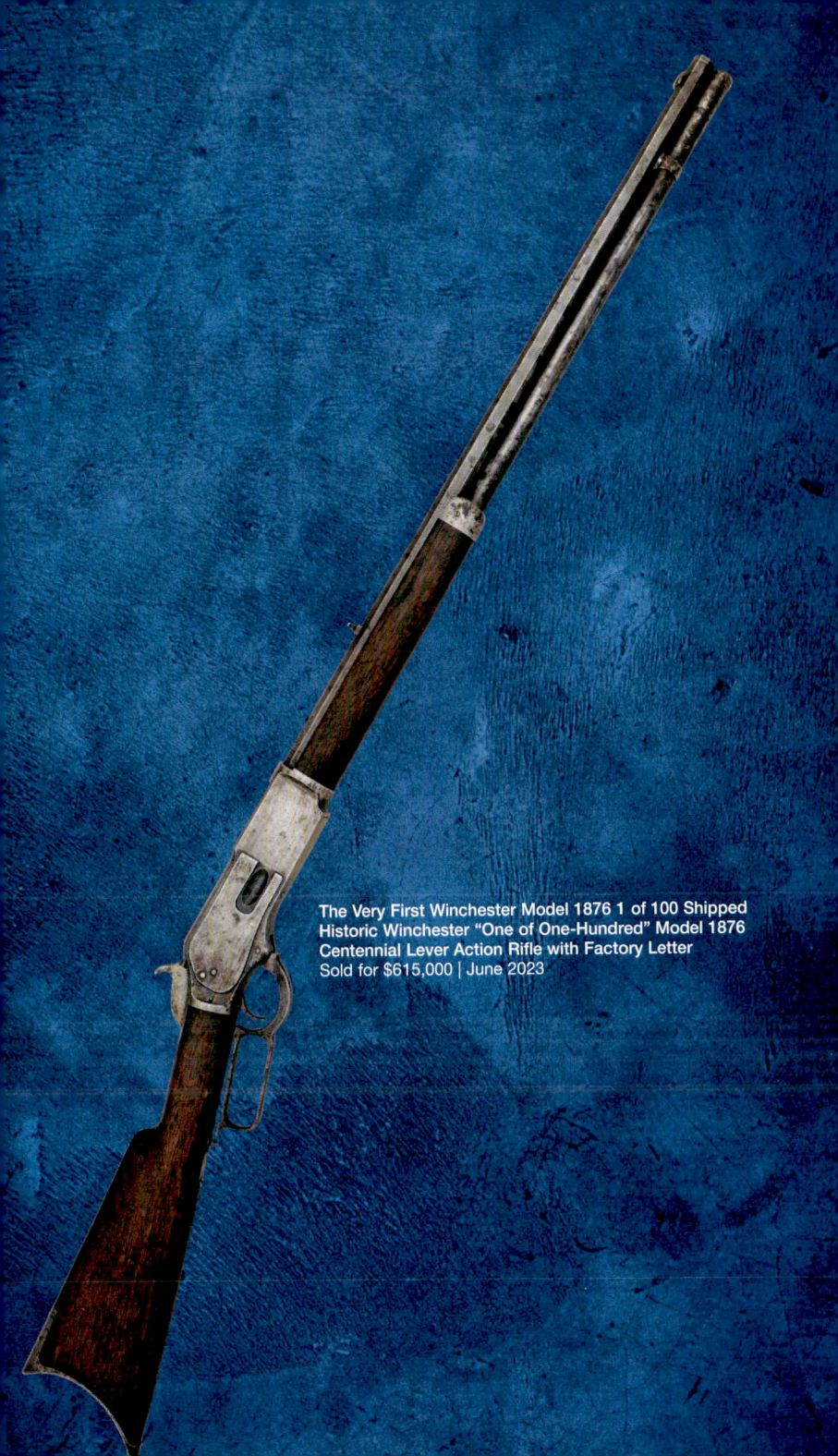

The Very First Winchester Model 1876 1 of 100 Shipped
Historic Winchester "One of One-Hundred" Model 1876
Centennial Lever Action Rifle with Factory Letter
Sold for $615,000 | June 2023

John F. Kennedy. White House Rocking Chair gifted by the President to former New York governor Averell Harriman.
Sold for $591,000 | May 2022
The Estate of Melvin "Pete" Mark, Jr.

since her late husband had worked so diligently on his collection for so many years, she assumed that the proceeds would enable her to afford a nice retirement in Florida.

We had to carefully explain that we couldn't help her with the sale of the coins. Her husband had enjoyed himself thoroughly for all those years, but he had never told her that he was spending more on holders, staples and boxes than he was on the coins. Her dreams of a luxurious retirement diminished, we advised her to contact two dealers who routinely purchase such coins. The fault was not in his collecting, but in his failure to inform his wife of the nature of the collection.

We more typically encounter surviving spouses and heirs at the other end of the spectrum. When your spouse spends $50,000 or $100,000 on rare coins or other collectibles, you generally have some knowledge of those purchases, but not always — and often, the most prodigious collectors are coy with their family about just how much they're investing. This leads to the more enjoyable surprises — those made-for-TV moments when we inform unsuspecting heirs of the vast fortune they've inherited.

Years ago we encountered the younger of two sisters who were dividing their father's estate. He had left Germany in the early 1930s — not a great time to immigrate to America, but an excellent time to be leaving Germany. He brought to America two collections: antique silver service pieces and his rare coins. The coins were sold mostly to establish his business in Iowa. Despite the hard times, he prospered and was able to devote the next 30 years to rebuilding his collection of German coins.

At the same time, he continued to expand his collection of 17th- and 18th-century German silverware. We knew every aspect of his collecting history because he left a meticulous record on index cards. Every coin and every piece of silver was detailed with his cataloging and purchase history. His daughter was in awe of his passion for maintaining such detailed records.

After his death, his daughters decided to split his collections between themselves. They added up the purchase values of each of his collections, which were just about equal. The older sister/executor had acquired some small knowledge of antique silver, and since she wished to keep all of the elegant heirloom tea service for herself, she decided to keep the silver and give her younger sister the coins

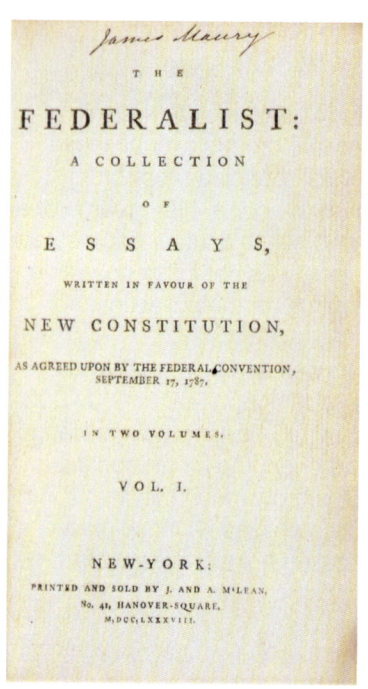

[Alexander Hamilton, James Madison, and John Jay]. *The Federalist: A Collection of Essays, Written in Favour of the New Constitution, as Agreed Upon by the Federal Convention, September 17, 1787.* New York: Printed and Sold by J. and A. M'Lean, 1788.
Sold for $312,500 | March 2020

— she definitely was not interested in splitting. After selling the non-family silver pieces through a regional auction house, she boasted of realizing more than $200,000 from her father's $27,000 investment.

The younger sister came to us with only one box of his coins. Her father's records for that box indicated a cost of less than $2,000, but knowing the years he had collected, we were anticipating at least a few nice coins. However, we were totally unprepared for what came next: pristine coins of the greatest rarity. His $2,000 box was worth more than $150,000, surpassing all our wildest expectations.

She then produced the record cards for the rest of the collection, and we offered to travel back to Iowa with her the same day. When we finished auctioning the coins, she had realized more than $1.2 million.

In another situation, the wife of a deceased coin dealer called us to consign $1 million in rare coins from his estate. This asset represented a significant portion of her retirement assets. We eagerly picked up the coins, and already had started cataloging and photographing when we received an urgent phone call from her attorney. The coins had to be returned immediately. It appeared that her husband had been holding the extensive coin purchases of his main customer in his vaults, and he had neither informed his wife nor adequately marked the boxes. Most of her $1 million retirement asset belonged to her husband's client and not to her husband.

A final example that really distressed us demonstrates that partial planning, no matter how well intentioned, cannot always guarantee the desired outcome. A collector with sizeable holdings divided his coins equally (by value) between his adult son and daughter, with instructions that they should seek expert advice before selling. After the daughter came to us, she was pleased to learn that her coins were worth in excess of $85,000.

Once she signed the Consignment Agreement, she told us the rest of the story. Her brother had "sold" his share eight months earlier to a local pawnbroker for less than $7,500. Her father hadn't shared his knowledge of the asset's value with his children for fear that his son would spend the money foolishly. Instead, her brother basically gave it away.

So, what should you do to prevent such problems?

If transferring your collection to the next generation is desirable, you will want to provide for an orderly transition. If they aren't interested in sharing your love of the collectibles, you will have to decide whether to dispose of the collection in your lifetime or leave that decision to your heirs. If the latter, your family should — at a minimum — have a basic understanding of your collection, its approximate value and how you want it distributed. The default do-nothing alternative can present a financial and emotional burden on your beneficiaries and lead to a costly estate settlement.

Important questions to be discussed:

- Are there heirs who will want the collection from a collector's standpoint?

- Where are the objects kept?

- Where is the inventory of the collectibles kept?

- What is the approximate value of the collection?

- Has the collection been appraised? Was the collection appraised by a qualified appraiser? Where is the appraisal and does it need to be updated?

- Do you have legal title to the collectibles in your possession? If the collectibles in your possession belong to someone else, do you have power as Agent, Trustee, Guardian, or Executor to deal with them?

- Are there certain dealers or other experts such as an auction house representative you trust to provide guidance to your heirs?

- Is there a firm that you and your heirs wish to use in the collection's disposition after your death? Is that firm noted somewhere in your estate plans?

The horror stories that begin this chapter are all true, none are isolated cases, and they won't be the last. If, for whatever reason, you choose not to to discuss your particular circumstances about the collection with your family, consider choosing a trusted person or estate planning professional to discuss your particular circumstances. You can also take the time to write detailed instructions or simply make notes in this book, and leave it in your safe deposit box or wherever you keep your valuables.

The next few chapters help guide you through your options for planning with collections. Whatever direction you and your family choose for the handling of your collection, the written instructions can be discussed with your estate planning advisor. Having thoughtful discussions with your advisor and family, along with a valid document stating your wishes kept with your collection's inventory, will greatly help your heirs when handling your estate.

1958 Mickey Mantle Game Worn New York Yankees Jersey, SGC Superior/Superior-Excellent with Multiple Photo Matches
Sold for $4,680,000 | August 2023

TIPS FOR HEIRS: This chapter does not address inheritance issues, but communications can be initiated from any direction. Do you have a parent with a collection? Certainly it is an issue that requires tact, but such a discussion may save considerable difficulty later. Additionally, if you know in advance that your spouse or relative has named you as executor in a will or as trustee of a trust, a few conversations about the collection will make your life much easier.

Chris Ivy's Story ....

Chris Ivy is the Director of Sports Auctions for Heritage Auctions. He graduated with a BA in History from the University of Texas at Austin and joined Heritage in 2001 after serving as a professional grader with Sportscard Guaranty Corporation (SGC) in New Jersey.

Heritage Auctions consignment director Peter Calderon was as skeptical of that first call as any reasonable person would have been: a hoard of 700 baseball cards that are more than 100 years old and in mint condition is something that never has happened before. So when a stranger calls you up and says that's what he has, it seems dubious.

But when he showed me the photos on his cell phone, I was intrigued. If it was what it looked like it was, this was a very, very big deal. The next day, the family sent us a box with eight cards via FedEx. We confirmed their authenticity and it would have been an amazing find even without the roughly 692 cards that still remained in Defiance, Ohio, where we flew as quickly as possible because the heirs were concerned about having that kind of value sitting in a home.

The consigner was a man named Karl Kissner, who, as the executor of his aunt's estate, represented some 30 heirs, each of whom had a stake in the collection. The cards had been stored in a box in an attic of the modest home for a century, buried under an antique dollhouse. One card had been out of the box during that time, exposed to the elements — and it served as a reminder of what would have happened to the other cards had they not been so well-preserved. But because of that box, we were staring at probably the single greatest find in the history of card collecting: ultra-rare cards depicting icons like Ty Cobb, Connie Mack, Cy Young and Honus Wagner, all in conditions similar to the brand-new cards you could buy today.

The question of how to sell the cards was challenging. At the time, the universe of collectors for the set likely consisted of a grand total of fewer than 50 people. The 1910 E-98 set was, paradoxically, so rare that few people wanted it. High-end early baseball card collectors tend to be relentless completionists — laser-focused on accumulating whole sets — and the E-98 set was so elusive that few collectors had ventured to try. The limited universe of collectors combined with the sheer size of the collection meant it would be financial suicide to try to sell the whole collection at once with a mega-auction.

Within the collectibles field, it is common for owners of hoards to sell off their treasures piecemeal over time, while keeping secret the true size of the collection out of fear that if people know how large it is, they would wait for the prices to come down. As a result, the prices never even start high.

With the family, we decided right away that wasn't the way to do it. First, we didn't think it was ethical — and that if we followed the "slow leak" approach, we would end up with a lot of disgruntled buyers who had overpaid for the first few cards only to watch the prices come down. Second, we knew that a cache of this size could attract tremendous media attention — especially if the family was willing to serve as the public face of it — and, with a set featuring a limited collector base like this one, we thought media attention could expand that market. We talked to the family about how to approach the press and the first questions were, "What should we call it? What's the name of the region you're from?" They told us it was known as The Black Swamp; at first, we weren't sure about calling it that. But while the name seemed a little dark, we decided that it was intriguing and mysterious enough to attract attention.

So we opted for a sort of hybrid approach. We would offer the story of The Black Swamp Find to the media, but also would carefully sell off the collection over the course of four or five years. We put out a press release, and the first major story came from The Associated Press. Local and cable news shows followed and, finally, the *Today Show* called. The story appeared on literally thousands of traditional and online media outlets.

Thirty members of the family came to the auction for the first few cards from the Black Swamp Find; in total, the first 30 cards we sold realized a combined $566,132. The family understands the importance of patience in realizing full value for the collection, so it looks like I'll be telling the story of the Black Swamp Find for years to come.

The Estate of
Mildred Hedrick Fender
Fort Worth, Texas

Heritage was honored to present an impressive collection of fine silver and decorative arts from the Estate of Mildred Hedrick Fender in our Fall 2022 auctions. Mildred's passion for giving back and her love of entertaining made her a pillar of the Fort Worth community.

John Bridge Silver Covered
Tureen on Stand,
London, 1827
Sold for $27,500

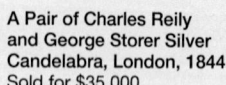

A Pair of Charles Reily
and George Storer Silver
Candelabra, London, 1844
Sold for $35,000

A Pair of Italian Marble Busts: *Minerva and Mars*, 18th century
Sold for $93,750

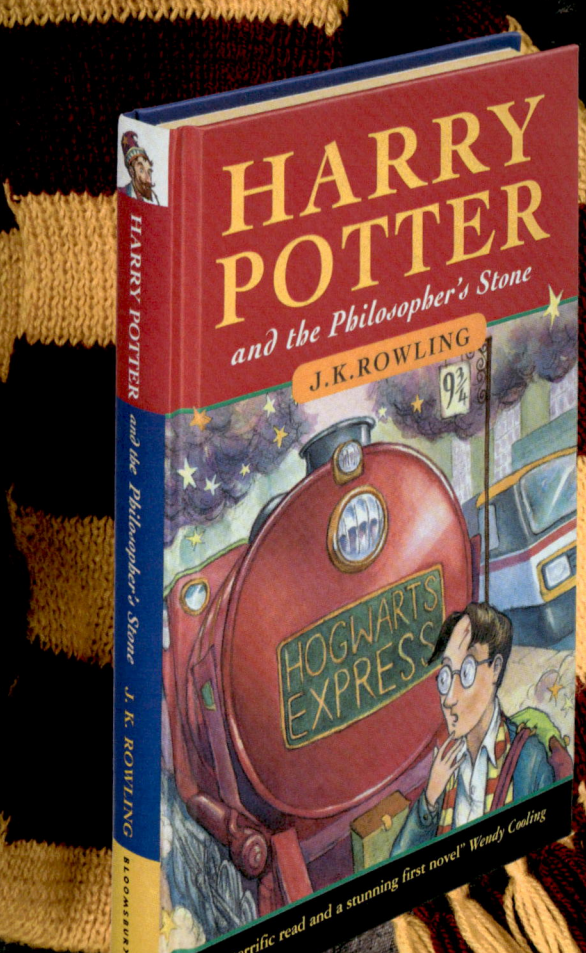

J. K. Rowling. *Harry Potter and the
Philosopher's Stone*. [London]:
Bloomsbury, [1997].
Sold for $471,000 | December 2021

5

Division of Assets

"There is a strange charm in the thoughts of a good legacy, or the hopes of an estate, which wondrously removes or at least alleviates the sorrow that men would otherwise feel for the death of friends." – Miguel De Cervantes

Inheritances bring out the best in some families and the worst in others. The problem is that it's difficult to predict exactly how the prospect of an inheritance will work out with any given family, so it's best to plan everything you possibly can in advance to minimize the potential for wrangling.

In the highly-charged, emotional environment surrounding the loss of a loved one, any weaknesses in the relationships of those left behind are exacerbated. Suspicious minds are more finely honed, and if the estate remains for the survivors to divide, it won't take much of a spark to ignite a fire. You can minimize the likelihood of family arguments, rifts and hurt feelings, as well as expensive and time-consuming litigation by seeking expert advice for your estate planning documents with precise written instructions for the division of your tangible assets to your heirs and beneficiaries. A separate writing listing your specific instructions for division and distribution can be helpful to serve as an adjunct to your estate planning documents. Make sure it is signed, dated, and the pages are numbered.

Instructions about collections are particularly important because they generally involve a large number of pieces with valuations that are not obvious based on appearance alone. For instance, in the world of coins and currency, the same coin and date can include a number of varieties and variations. Without the help of an expert, it is not difficult to make an expensive error.

Upon a collector's death, the representative of the estate, usually the trustee or executor, will have the duty of getting the collection appraised by a qualified appraiser to establish Fair Market Value (FMV) as of the date of death. This valuation creates a new tax cost basis to use in the future when selling or gifting the collection.

The values of items in a collection should not be based on insurance appraisals; when this mistake is made, the heir who receives the collection can come out far behind heirs who receive cash or real estate. Insurance appraisals usually represent a "retail replacement" valuation that can be very different from the "fair market" valuation that would be used for financial planning or estate tax purposes. "Fair market valuations" represent, by definition, a value closer to what a collection might be expected to bring in an orderly sale.

Omega, Very Rare And Important Gold Speedmaster Professional Wristwatch, No. 19, Presented To Astronaut Michael Collins, circa 1969
The Estate of Michael Collins
Sold for $765,000 | June 2022

John Lennon Personally Owned and Used Pair of Reading Glasses.
Sold for $57,500 | December 2021

If an appraisal is not necessary to the estate administration, auction houses can be a good resource for "auction estimates." These are not the same as an appraised FMV determination. They are a realistic estimate of what an item could sell for an the open market, and most auction houses provide this service free of charge. Your legal advisor should always be the resource of whether a formal appraisal or auction estimates are needed for your estate administration.

It may be disheartening to learn that your family members do not share your passion and level of interest in your collection. Collectors incorporate multiple strategies into their estate plans to achieve a desired outcome. A simpler alternative is to establish an estate plan directing that the articles be sold, with the proceeds shared equally among the heirs rather than family members dealing with the process of equitably dividing a collection.

Even with the best planning, you may still have the dilemma of whether it is better for you to sell or dispose of your collection during your lifetime or at death. During your lifetime, your personal knowledge and management has served you well. We suggest you take care and consideration by seeking advice from various professionals - an auction house with whom you've worked well, or your wealth, legal, and tax advisors. This will assist you in making a personal decision that will serve your desires and preserve the asset value and family dynamic.

A number of tax issues, which will be discussed later, also must be considered. For now, it's important to remember that there are different tax consequences related to sales and gifts during your lifetime versus disposition at your death. However, taxes should only be a part of your determination — not the sole consideration. You must weigh many factors in deciding what is best for you and your family.

In summary, your collection is yours to enjoy now and yours to sell or give away as you see fit. The old saw says, "You can't take it with you." You can, however, ensure that the collection provides as much value for others as it has for you.

Make an action plan for your collection, even if you anticipate many more decades of collecting.

If the timing is immediate, speak to your legal, tax and financial advisors who are essential to the implementation of your plan and are equipped to proceed accordingly. Otherwise, prepare detailed written instructions and leave copies with both your collection and your estate plan. If you prefer that your collectibles be distributed among family members, provide specific instructions in writing as to how distribution is to be accomplished. If you wish to distribute the proceeds, providing a preference for a firm or dealer who is knowledgeable, trustworthy, and reputable is always helpful.

With tax laws becoming more complex and ever changing, it is wise to review your estate plan annually with your advisors. This can help assure that your wishes for your collection are accurately and effectively managed.

TIPS FOR HEIRS: Good communication between family members can go a long way to enhance a good estate plan and ease the transfer of assets. Involvement in a parent's collecting activities can create new and lasting bonds between the family members; you may even begin to enjoy collecting yourself.

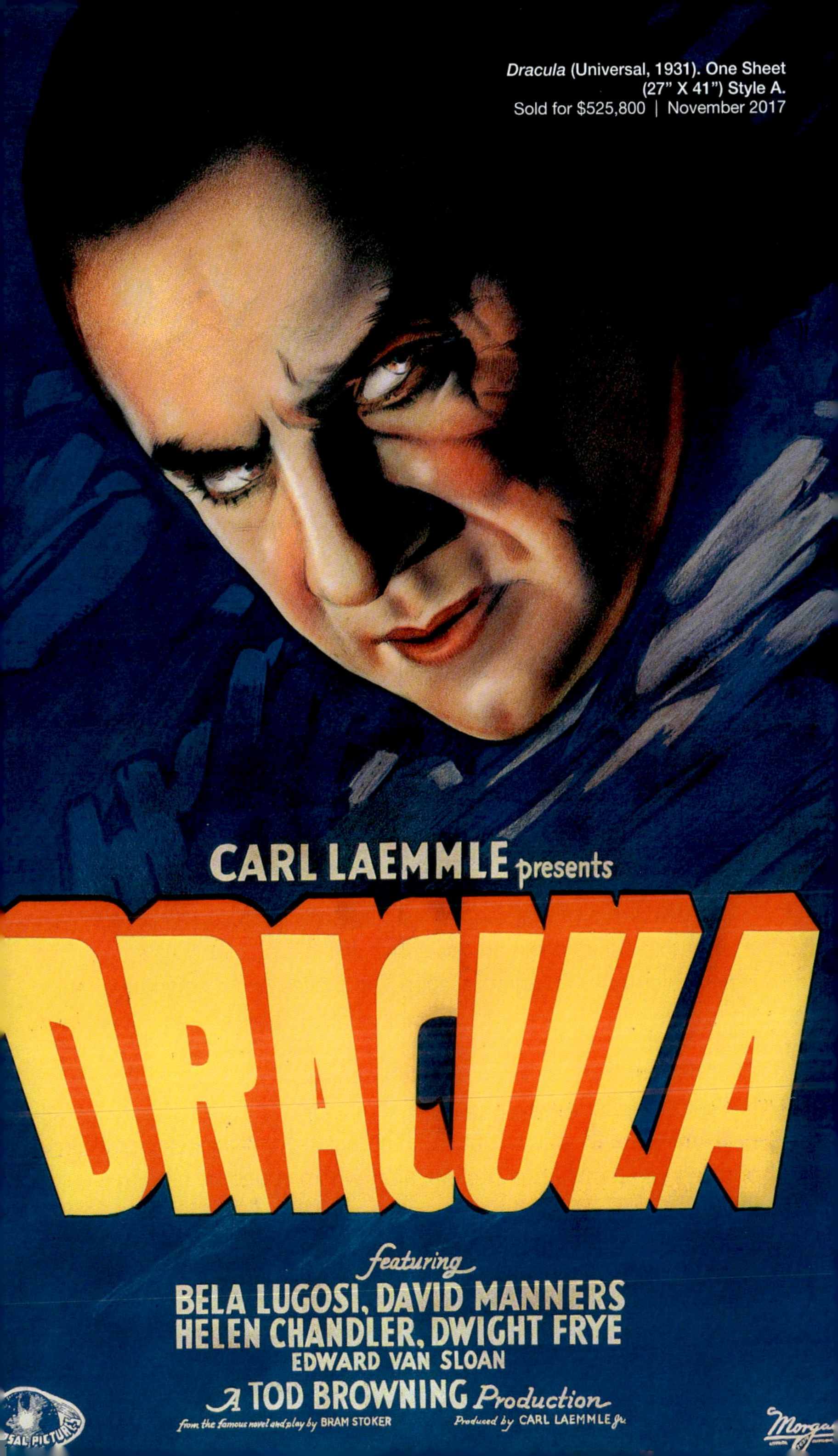

Dracula (Universal, 1931). One Sheet (27" X 41") Style A.
Sold for $525,800 | November 2017

How Heritage Set a New Market for Norman Rockwell Preliminary Studies By Pitting Different Category Collectors Against Each Other

In 2016, an iconic but very small 11.5" x 9.25" Rockwell study — paint sketched onto a photographic print — for his famous painting *Triple Self Portrait*, was offered to Heritage Senior Vice-President Ed Jaster by a previous consignor of minor Rockwell works. The client was successful with his other offerings and Heritage was his first call. Heritage estimated the piece at $150,000-$250,000. "This seemed to be a realistic price at the time," said Jaster, "based on its size and the fact that a similarly sized study for Rockwell's also-iconic Girl with Black Eye had failed to sell the previous year at Sotheby's against a $200,000-$300,000 estimate."

Eventually, the owner of the art chose Heritage, partly based on a recommendation by an independent Rockwell specialist, and partly based on his previous success with his consignment to Heritage. He believed that Heritage would be the best auction house to recruit collectors across the spectrum of collecting categories rather than just marketing the work to art buyers. According to Jaster, "It had long been Heritage's view that our top clients, regardless of specific collecting focus, maintain a great interest in iconic artworks and collectibles in any category. This insight informs our promotion efforts and gives our consignors a major advantage over those of other leading auction houses."

After substantial advertising and public relations campaigns, the day of the auction found multiple bidders competing. The field comprised not only American Art and Illustration Art collectors, but major Coin collectors and serious Comic Art collectors, all of whom ended up battling it out.

These bidders drove the price to set a new record for any Rockwell study at an unprecedented $1,322,500, becoming the first Rockwell study to reach seven figures. The winner was a noted Comics and Illustration Art collector, and the under-bidder was primarily a Comics Art client.

Norman Rockwell (American, 1894-1978)
Study for Triple Self Portrait, 1960
Sold for $1,332,500 | May 2017

Coincidentally, just weeks later, another major Rockwell study larger in size (16" x 15") showed up at Heritage Auctions' offices addressed to our Sports Collectible department. Its arrival was completely unrelated to *Triple Self Portrait*. Indeed, the owners, descended from the umpire at the center of the image, believed they were sending us an autographed print worth just a few thousand dollars. To that family's delight, Heritage specialists quickly identified the so-called print as an original painted cover study for the 1948 baseball-themed Saturday Evening Post cover dubbed *Tough Call*.

"In a controversial decision even within the company," Jaster continued, "our team decided to run the painting in our fall 2017 Online Signature Sports Auction, this time with an estimate of $300,000-up. Would lightning strike twice?"

Indeed it would! The fields of Fine Art, Illustration Art and Sports collectors ran the study up to a new record of $1.68 million in an Internet-only bidding war, which was ultimately won by a Sports collector.

As further evidence of the depth of Heritage's cross-marketing efforts, the two winning bidders as well as the two direct under-bidders of each lot consisted of four separate clients.

Norman Rockwell (American, 1894-1978)
Tough Call, Saturday Evening Post cover study (detail), April 23, 1949
1948 Original Study for "Tough Call" by Norman Rockwell –
Gifted to Legendary Umpire "Beans" Reardon.
Sold for $1,680,000 | August 2017

WORLD AUCTION RECORD FOR AN OIL STUDY BY THE ARTIST

Keith Haring (1958-1990)
Andy Mouse, 1986
Portfolio of 4 screenprints in colors on
Lenox Museum Board
Edition 1 of 30
Sold for $945,000 October 2023
Private Collection, Miami, Florida

6

Should You Bequeath Your Collection, or Sell During Your Lifetime?

"The main thing is to be moved, to love, to hope, to tremble, to live."
– Auguste Rodin

A collector spends countless hours of their time carefully and lovingly amassing a collection, often having fought for individual pieces at auctions, made great discoveries in unlikely locales, overpaid for that much needed example and watched as the value of that collection grew over the years. Selling a collection during the collector's lifetime can provide enjoyment, accolades and the benefit of reaping the financial rewards. That financial realization can be used for donations, gifts or to pursue building a better collection — or beginning in a whole new collecting field. As collectors ourselves, we understand the fun of collecting and the pleasure to be found in the thrill of the hunt. We see many collectors who sell an entire collection multiple times during their lives and then branch into wildly fluctuating directions of interest — or choose to concentrate their collecting on higher quality examples in their field.

First, let's consider some of the logistical and practical reasons for selling a collection during one's lifetime rather than donating, gifting or leaving the collection in your estate.

Start planning for your collection early if you want it preserved, or if you want your heirs to receive the highest value for it, even if you anticipate many more decades of collecting. Research and stay informed regarding the current market for your collecting category to know when it might be the best time to sell or when it appears to be more of a buyer's market.

A collector may have established relationships with a particular auction house or dealer — or have strong opinions as to what venue they would prefer to see their collection sold through. Being able to make the decision of sale venue and negotiate the best possible sale terms should be the responsibility and concern of the collector themselves, not left as a burden to their heirs. All too often we see situations where inherited collections or disinterested families sell in inadequate local venues or to unscrupulous dealers and receive only a small percentage of the true value. Below is an example of how much can go wrong when there is a lack of careful planning during a collector's lifetime:

> *Heritage's Trusts & Estates Department was approached by an heir who had inherited half of his father's comic book collection and wanted to know what the sale potential and market value was for his inheritance. The comics turned out to be wonderful examples of some rare and excellent condition Golden and Silver Age comics from the 1940s through 1960s. Heritage marketed the collection extensively and ended up selling the comics at auction for over $800,000. When we asked the heir about the other half of the collection that had been left to his sibling, he told us the all-too-familiar story of the other half having been sold locally for less than $15,000. His sibling's disinterest and lack of knowledge about the value potential for the collection resulted in a significant loss of inheritance — surely not their father's intention.*

Mandatory or precatory language can be included in your testamentary documents (Trusts, Wills, codicils) or attached through directives to instruct trustees, executors, personal representative and heirs how you would prefer your collection to be dispersed or sold as part of your estate. Mandatory provisions must be followed but precatory language in directives generally are unenforceable and could be ignored. Depending on your intentions, one may be better than the other and the right option should be discussed with your attorney or other advisors. Heritage Auctions' Trusts and Estate team can also provide some guidance on the advantages and disadvantages of each.

Transfer of Collections - To Gift or not to Gift

Federal law imposes a tax on transfers of assets during life and after death, and an additional tax on transfers to grandchildren and more remote individuals. That said, federal law provides a unified tax structure for lifetime transfers and transfers after death and is indexed for inflation. The current (calendar year 2025) lifetime gift tax or estate tax exemption threshold, the amount over which a gift tax or estate tax would apply, is $13.99 million per

A Rare and Large Chinese Underglaze Copper Red Peony Dish, Ming Dynasty, Hongwu Period
Sold for $275,000 September 2022
Property from the Estate of Dr. Cornelius Osgood and Soo Sui-ling Osgood

A Pair of Chinese Cloisonné Lions with Riders, 18th century
Sold for $175,000 | September 2023
Property from the Estate of Mrs. Amon G. Carter, Jr., Fort Worth, Texas

Porfirio Salinas (American, 1910-1973)
Blue and Gold
Sold for $42,500 | October 2022
Property from a Texas Estate

individual, or $27.98 million for a married couple. It should be noted that 15 states have an estate tax and 6 states have an inheritance tax (with one having both), but only Connecticut has a gift tax. State exemption are lower than the federal exemptions, meaning if you live in a state with an estate or inheritance tax, your assets may still be subject to tax even if your total estate is less than the federal exemption threshold.

If a collector has total assets in excess of the gift/estate tax threshold, then consideration should be given to the tax implications of holding appreciating assets until death as opposed to disposing of them by sale, gift, charitable donation or otherwise during life. The issue regarding timing of how and when to transfer or dispose of assets is complex and should be considered in consultation with a collecting consultant and your tax or other financial advisors.

A non-tax consideration for lifetime gifting is the intangible value of seeing your assets used and appreciated by the recipient during life. Among the tax considerations would be getting any future appreciation in the value of an asset out of your taxable estate. The considerations involved in making lifetime gifts or gifts at death require careful planning and analysis with family members, estate, and tax advisors to ensure your wishes and expectations are met for your collection.

What is the benefit of using the $13.99 million lifetime gift exemption - $27.98 million with a spousal gift plan -- in your lifetime, rather than wait until death and use your estate tax exemption? With property that has a good chance of appreciating substantially in the future, gifting it during life removes its value from your taxable estate and you will eliminate any future appreciation in these assets from your estate.

For example, you decide to gift a painting in 2025 with a fair market value of $5 million. This amount is removed from your taxable estate with the completed gift. Upon your death, the painting's fair market value is $8 million. With the painting being removed from your estate due to the gift in 2025, it is not taxable as part of your estate and no tax is due on the $3 million in appreciation after the gift. By careful planning with lifetime gifts, especially appreciating assets, not only can you share something meaningful sooner with the gift recipient, you can also save estate taxes by removing any appreciation of that asset after making the gift.

In addition to no state taxes on lifetime gifts (other than for Connecticut residents), every individual is able to make gifts up to the annual exclusion amount each calendar year. The 2025 annual gift exclusion amount is $19,000. An individual can make as many annual gifts to as many people (not just family) as they wish during a tax year. For married individuals, that amount is double either by the spouse making their own gifts or simply treating the gifted amount as a split gift. If gifting hard to value assets, such as collectibles, or making gifts to anyone individual in excess of the annual exclusion amount, make sure to consult with your tax advisor to determine what, if any, reporting is required.

When considering gifting, there are some important tax considerations, such as how lifetime giving affects the tax cost basis of the gifted item. For tax purposes, the cost basis is the original purchase price of an asset (referred to as "carryover basis"). Generally, a taxpayer who acquires property by gift takes a basis in the property equal to the donor's adjusted basis in the property at the time of the gift. While the basis usually remains the same as the original owner, the basis may be adjusted to account for any gift taxes that were paid at the time of the gift. To figure out the basis of the property received as a gift, you must know the donor's adjusted basis at the time of the fair market value of the property at the time the donor made the gift, and the amount of any gift tax, if any, paid on the gift. As noted above, no gift tax would be due unless total lifetime gifts exceeds the then available exclusion amount.

Donation Considerations

The notion of preserving one's legacy for future generations in the public collections of museums, libraries and archives, is every collector's dream. Unfortunately, the reality of what might happen to your beloved collection upon donation may not reflect your intent and expectations.

Museums and non-profits may not need or desire your beloved collection. For example: in order for a collector to receive the optimum tax benefits of a donation, the receiving entity must have "related and like use" of the items. A collector's perception of the importance of works of art or collectibles may not be shared by current or future curators. The museum's mission and direction may change over the years so that your donation may find its way into a storage cabinet or warehouse locker.

A museum's permanent collection is not always permanent, and museums are a consistent source of material in the auction market. Whether sold to fund future acquisitions, assist with the wider capital campaigns, or even provide operating funds, institutions often have a more pressing need for money than objects. In many cases, it is preferable for the institution to receive a cash donation over an individual's collection.

In addition, donating the cash from a sale of an item doesn't often generate the same concern for an IRS audit as does a tangible gift which requires an appraisal. An auction sale almost always complies with the very definition of fair market value and determines the charitable donation valuation for tax purposes. Past abuses, including outright fraud and tax evasion, have led to very strict requirements for acceptable charitable donation appraisals, which are more fully explained in the appraisal chapter of this book.

Many institutions do not accept donations that are bound by stipulations of permanent holding or display. Only a very small percentage of donated items actually get displayed. Furthermore, when a particular painting or artifact becomes especially valuable in the market, the decision may be made to sell it in order to obtain the monetary funds to support the institution's mission and endeavors.

If the institution is requesting the gift or donation from you, the object probably has a much better chance of regular exhibition, although there is never a long-term guarantee. If the donated item is regularly displayed, it usually will have acknowledgement of the donation's source on the wall plaque and in any published literature. There are other methods in gifting a tangible asset that can provide the same recognition but under different circumstances. For example, a collector may consider loaning a piece of art to an institution or a fractional gift of ownership. Including art or collectibles as part of museum exhibitions adds to the provenance or history of a piece, which will make it that much more desirable and valuable to the market.

Auctioning a collection in its entirety can increase the value of the lesser pieces in the collection by association with the most sought-after pieces. By establishing a collection identity, the provenance and pedigree of that collection will carry forward with the items forevermore to add recognition and appreciation both for the collector and the collection. Particularly in the collectible categories such as coins and comic books, the provenance and pedigree is key to securing an item's desirability and value in the market.

The idea of parting with a beloved collection may seem initially unwelcomed and unthinkable, but the fact is that the "letting go" of a collection is an inevitable part of a collector's life — the question is how and when. With proper planning by a team of professional advisors, making wise decisions to oversee and control the sale, gift or donation can lead to greater after-tax monetary reward, family harmony and fulfilling charitable objectives.

**Disneyland - Original Club 33 Sign
(Walt Disney, c. 1967).**
Sold for $108,000 | May 2022

A Decision to Sell ··············The Gardner Collection

When it comes to selling a collection that was assembled over years as a labor of love, many collectors like to have a hand in the process, using the sale as a way to document their connection to the items under their care and to share the stories behind them.

In total, the over 3,000 coins in the collection of Pennsylvania collector Eugene H. Gardner brought more than $53 million across four major auctions at Heritage between 2014 and 2015.

The collection was the product of a keen eye and a passion for numismatics that began in 1954 when as a college student Gardner began assembling his first coin collection. That collection was sold in 1965 but Gardner soon caught the collecting bug again. The resulting "second collection" was widely considered by numismatic experts to be among the finest collections of silver coinage ever assembled. Gardner said he learned many lessons when putting together his first collection, then applying these in his second collecting effort.

For Gardner, it was important for him to work with Heritage in the presentation of his collection, since he viewed the auctions as the culmination of a gratifying and absorbing collecting career. Gardner said that the sale of his collection "allows me to introduce my largely completed collection to the numismatic fraternity, which is very exciting to me. I love the thought of sharing the auction experience with my family. We've really all been in this together. In fact, my grandchildren know how to get my attention by just saying, 'Opa, what new coins do you have?'"

1802 Half Dime
AU50 PCGS
Sold for $352,500 | June 2017

The Gardner Collection

His decision to sell his collection across a series of Heritage sales over the course of a year, rather than at a single auction, served multiple purposes — all in the interest of maximizing the sale totals. First, it allowed collectors and dealers to stretch out their bidding dollars instead of having to use all of their funds at one time. Second, the strategy allowed key parts of the collector's groups of early U.S. silver coins, Barber coins and Seated Liberty material to be spread out fairly evenly. Gardner purchased many of his coins at auction, making the prices that he paid public record. By establishing a new price point, he would allow for even higher prices in the subsequent auctions.

Looking at the results of the Gardner sales shows that many coins went up in value, a few went down, and some went unchanged in their trips to the auction block. A collection's success at auction needs to be looked at as a whole, because at auction, anything can happen with a single lot. Success is best measured by how well a collection does in total for the collection as a whole.

Gardner's 1802 Draped Bust half dime, graded an About Uncirculated 50, was a highlight. As Heritage's catalog noted, "One of the most desirable coins in high grade in the Gardner Collection, the 1802 half dime is a signal rarity, a 'trophy coin' for even the most advanced numismatist and an issue unknown in Mint State."

It sold at a 2009 Heritage auction for $195,500 (then graded by the Professional Coin Grading Service as an Extremely Fine 45). At the first Gardner auction on June 23, 2014, the piece (upgraded to an About Uncirculated 50) sold for a strong $352,500, that price serving as a testament to the quality and rarity of the piece. Heritage worked with Gardner to help maximize value in his collection by seeking upgrades when possible. The result was that Gardner, and his legacy as a collector, will survive for generations in the many coins that carry the Gardner pedigree.

1959 Gibson Les Paul Standard
Sunburst Solid Body Electric Guitar,
Serial #9 0696
Sold for $350,000 | July 2021

7

Collectibles, Estate Planning and Taxes

"The only difference between death and taxes is that death doesn't get worse every time Congress meets." – Will Rogers

If you are an avid collector, your collection may represent a large portion of your net worth and your estate. While your real estate, stocks, bonds, and other traditional investments are probably accounted for in your estate plan, your collection may not be. It is important to ensure that your Estate Planning Advisory Team knows the type, size and approximate value of your collection. The inclusion of these assets in your estate could make a difference in how your team constructs your estate plan, what tax advantages they obtain, and what tax liabilities they can mitigate.

When a person dies owning property, that property is transferred to a recipient. The process of determining the recipients of those assets— who gets what, when they get it, and what will be done about taxes—is the central purpose of estate planning. The decisions you make can have a significant impact on the amount of ordinary income, capital gains, gift and/or estate taxes that you or your heirs will pay. Since we cannot know the particulars in your case, we cannot advise you about which of these planning options to use and how they apply to your personal situation. We recommend that you review our information to inform yourself in advance of reviewing the plan with your professional estate and wealth advisors.

We strongly recommend that your advisor team should include a legal professional, preferably an attorney who is specializing in estate planning and/or probate law, other tax advisor, preferably a CPA, a financial advisor and, in some instances, a life insurance professional.

Tax and estate planning laws can be extremely complex. Decisions about the benefits and detriments of making lifetime gifts, or gifts by will or trust, and whether life insurance should play a role in your planning, requires careful analysis by trained professionals. If your

1804 $10 Plain 4, BD-2, JD-1,
Judd-33, High R.7,
PR65+ Deep Cameo PCGS. CAC
Sold for $5,280,000 | January 2021
The Bob R. Simpson Collection

advisory team is made up of the right combination of individuals, between you and your advisory team, you should be able to create the plan that best suits your unique needs and wishes. Changes in income tax laws can also influence your decision making. For example, long-term capital gains on collectibles are currently taxed at a rate of 28 percent or your marginal tax rate, whichever is lower, while long-term capital gains on other assets, like your stocks or real estate, are generally taxed at a lower rate of 15 or 20 percent. This was not always the case and could change depending on the tax policy of any particular administration in the future.

Between you and your advisory team, you should be able to create the plan that best suits your unique needs and wishes. Tax and estate planning laws can be extremely complex and there is no single individual who can be relied upon to advise you on all aspects of the legal, tax and insurance matters that are involved in estate planning. As we stated before, tax laws are always changing and have significant impact on the taxation of your estate, and on decisions about the benefits and detriments of making lifetime gifts, or gifts by will or trust. For example, long-term capital gains on collectibles are currently taxed at a rate of 28 percent or your marginal tax rate, whichever is lower, while long-term capital gains on other assets, like your stocks or real estate, are generally taxed at a lower rate of 15 or 20 percent.

Annual gifts of up to $19,000 (since 2025) may be made by you to as many individuals as you choose without affecting your lifetime gift/estate exemption. If your spouse joins you in the gift, you can distribute $38,000 each year to as many lucky recipients as you choose, without reducing your joint lifetime exemption. In addition, as of 2025, you are allowed a $13.99 million lifetime gift/estate exemption, ($27.98 million with your spouse/partner).

Is Your Collection Worth More Today Than When You Purchased It?

As with any carefully chosen investment, a collection should hopefully appreciate in value over time. There are, of course, exceptions.

If you were unfortunate enough to have been the victim of an unscrupulous seller, or perhaps acquired some of your collectibles at the peak of a market that has since declined, a current appraisal may indicate that you are in a capital loss position. If that's the case, you may sell the collection and use the loss to offset an equal amount of capital gains. In addition, you may deduct up to $3,000 annually ($1,500 if you are married and filing separately) of excess capital losses against your ordinary income. These losses may be carried forward to future years until they are entirely used, or until your death.

Certain losses, depending on their character (short- or long-term) may offset only certain gains and the IRS has established a priority for offsetting short- and long-term capital gains. The best strategy when you incur capital gains that can't be offset with losses is to simply pay the tax. If the collection has appreciated, many other issues come into play. These are discussed over the next few pages.

The Unpredictability of the Estate Tax

Unless you have successfully completed your lifetime planning, many of the assets held directly in your name will transfer into your estate upon your death. Your estate will have to pay estate taxes if the net value is greater than the exemption amount set by Congress. Unfortunately, Congress has made planning for the estate tax challenging by continually changing the size of the exemption.

If you bequeath a large estate of tangible assets to your heirs, without proper planning, your heirs may require a substantial amount of liquid funds to satisfy the estate taxes.

Without extensions, estate taxes must be paid to the government in cash within nine months of death. Often, the unfortunate result of this immediate need for cash will be a "fire sale" to raise the required funds by the tax filing date. A hasty sale will not maximize the value of the collection to which you have devoted a great amount of time and effort. Despite your best intentions, your heirs may not benefit from your collection as you had intended without proper planning.

One part of the solution to the need of immediate liquidity to pay for potential estate taxes can be life insurance.

First, you will need your accountant or advisor to develop a pro forma balance sheet and income statement to determine the extent of the potential estate tax liability based upon the best estimate of the value of your estate at some future date. Depending on the valuation of your

Julian Onderdonk (American, 1882-1922)
Texas Landscape with Bluebonnets
Oil on canvas
Sold for $437,000 | November 2015

estate, your advisor can estimate the amount of tax that may be due upon your passing.

This part of your planning is more of an art than a science. The value of your assets, which may appreciate or depreciate over time, is somewhat unpredictable. Because one's date of death is uncertain, the tax rates that will apply are uncertain. Based on these assumptions, your advisor should be able to assist you in determining the tax consequences of making lifetime gifts compared with making bequests at the time of your passing as directed in your estate plan. These assumptions will also determine the various strategies that are available to reduce your tax liabilities.

If structured properly, life insurance policy's proceeds will not be included in your estate. This is generally accomplished by placing the ownership of the policy in a separate trust (an irrevocable life insurance trust, or "ILIT" for short) or having the policy directly owned by a third party. Upon your death, the proceeds of the policy are payable immediately in cash and pass to the trust beneficiaries or policy beneficiaries free of income and estate taxes.

How much life insurance you need and how to pay the premiums for such insurance can be complicated. Funding an ILIT usually entails gifting cash or income generating assets to the trust. While the goal of life insurance is usually income replacement and/or addressing liquidity needs, the exact amount necessary should be determined in consultation with planners and financial advisors. For collectors with significant holdings, they may want to insure the full tax liability of their collections to ensure that their collections can remain intact for family enjoyment and legacy holding. Without proper liquidity, a hasty sale could be required to raise proper capital to pay estate tax obligations.

The Gift Tax and Reducing Your Estate through Annual Gifting

Especially in light of the onerous estate tax rates that can inflict substantial damage on your estate (40 percent on all amounts above your available exemption amount), reducing your taxable estate through annual gifts to your heirs during your lifetime is a simple and extremely advantageous strategy, if implemented properly. As a general principle, a gift is any gratuitous transfer or a transfer by sale for less than the fair market value of the transferred asset.

The gift tax applies to completed transfers of assets during your lifetime to individuals or present interests to trusts in excess of the annual exclusion applicable to gifts in any one year. As previously discussed, our current tax law provides for annual gifts of $19,000 per recipient (for 2025), or $38,000 per individual for married couples. Current law allows you to make gifts of present interest to any number of recipients. In addition, certain gifts are not considered taxable gifts, including medical and educational expenses that you directly pay for someone, gifts to your spouse (if your spouse is not a US citizen, the amount that can be given tax free is limited) and gifts to a political organization for its use.

If gifts are made other than by cash, an appraisal of the property may be necessary and appropriate. If the gift exceeds the annual exclusion, and total gifts are in excess of the lifetime exemption amount, as a general rule, the donor is responsible for the payment of any taxes that are due on the gift. There may be times that the donor wants the beneficiary to pay the gift tax in which case the tax on the gift is based on a formula and results in a lower effective tax rate.

1875 $10 AU53 PCGS
Sold for $1,020,000 | October 2022
The Estate of Allan H. Goldman

Sean Scully (b. 1945)
Lipari, 1990
Oil on linen
Sold for $495,000 | November 2021
Property of a Chicago Collector

If your gift exceeds the then available annual exclusion to any person during the year, you must report it on a gift tax return (IRS Form 709). Spouses splitting gifts in excess of the annual exclusion for an individual generally must also file Form 709, even when no taxable gift is due. Once you give more than the annual gift tax exclusion, you begin to reduce your lifetime gift and estate tax exemption. When you pass away, your available exemption for estate tax purposes will be net of your lifetime taxable gifts. .

There are additional opportunities when it comes to transfers between spouses. Under current law you may gift an unlimited amount of property during your lifetime to a spouse without paying gift tax as long as your marriage is legally recognized, your spouse is a U.S. citizen and the gift is not through an irrevocable trust. Similarly, upon your death, the marital deduction allows you to pass an unlimited amount of property to your spouse tax-free. It should be noted that marital transfers merely defer estate taxes — they do not eliminate them. However, using the marital deduction to equalize the estates of both spouses, when appropriate, will allow you to maximize your estate tax exemptions by transferring assets between the two of you. The legal and practical implications of any such planning should be discussed with your trusted advisors.

The use of annual and lifetime gifts is an essential part of any estate plan. It's not exciting, but it is important. At a minimum, you now have a basic understanding of the concepts to enable you to ask the appropriate questions of your advisors.

Fractional Gifting Considerations

Collectors who want to make gifts of individual items that have a value greater than the $19,000 annual exclusion amount have another tax saving tool available. Consider the use of fractional gifting over time, either directly or through establishing beneficiary trusts. Gifting a percentage of the ownership — and thus value — of an item allows for the retention of the piece by the collector while lowering the taxable estate to more manageable and advantageous amounts each year. A $19,000 fractional gift to a few family members annually may equal just a small percentage of the value of an object or collection. However, over a number of years or even decades, collectors can make full use of their tax-exempt gift allowances if planning begins early.

The Capital Gains Tax

Everything you own for investment purposes is a capital asset. This includes any investment properties you have, stocks and bonds, mutual funds, and collections—if you bought them with an eye toward investment.

When you sell a capital asset, the difference between the price you paid for it (known as your cost basis) and the amount you sell it for is a capital gain or capital loss. If you held the asset for more than a year before selling, it is considered long-term. If you held the asset for less than a year, it is short-term..

The cost basis of an asset depends upon how you acquired the asset. If you purchased the asset, the basis is the amount you paid at the time of purchase, including but not limited to any associated expenses, such as commissions, fees and improvements to the property, etc. If you received the property as a gift, the basis usually is the price that the donor making the gift originally paid for it, which also is called the "carryover basis." If you inherited the asset upon the death of the donor, your basis is the fair market value of the asset at the date of death, called a "stepped-up basis."

Capital gains on most assets held for more than one year are subject to federal tax at a lower rate than ordinary income. The capital gains for asset held for more than a year (long-term capital gains) are generally taxed at a maximum of 20 percent on most assets. Collectible, such as coins, fine art, comics, or rare books, however, are taxed at a maximum rate of 28 percent. If your marginal income tax rate is below 28 percent, your gain on the sale of collectibles will be taxed at the marginal rate; if your marginal rate is above 28 percent, your gain will be taxed at 28 percent — providing you with some tax savings, but not nearly what you would get with investments in stocks or bonds. Assets held less than a year are deemed short-term, with short-term capital gains taxed at ordinary income tax rates (this is true for all investments, from stocks and bonds to more obscure collectible investments).

Trusts

The most commonly used trust is the living trust. In legal terms, it is known as a "revocable living trust." In simple terms, the living trust is a document that is used in conjunction with a will, but can avoid the costs and time involved in probating a will. In addition, while probate and settlement of Wills are public, trusts are private documents and third parties are not entitled to know the contents of trusts. Using a trust to pass assets to your spouse, children and others, allows you to put conditions on how assets are used and distributed. In addition, in the event you would like your spouse to enjoy your assets during their life but ensure the assets pass to specific individuals or groups upon their death, a properly structured trust could help delay the payment of taxes, if your estate is otherwise taxable, until the death of your spouse.

If you decide to place your collection into a trust, work with an experienced estate planning attorney to draft the trust document. When using a Trust as the centerpiece of your estate plan, a will is also drafted to supplement the trust as a failsafe to pick up any assets that were not transferred into your trust (retitled) prior to your death. It is important to note, only assets that have been retitled in the name of the trust, or otherwise properly deemed transferred to the Trust, will help avoid the need to open a probate to transfer asset to the Trust and your heirs. Once your collection is held in a trust, the trust document will dictate how your collection is managed. Using art as an example, in the trust provisions, you can allocate certain works of art to specific individuals or direct the trustee to select which beneficiaries receive or use certain works of art. By utilizing a trust for your collection, you can allow your beneficiaries to enjoy the collection without giving them full control over collection thus preserving your legacy.

While you are alive, you may be the trustee of your revocable trust and maintain complete control of the assets. When you pass away, the successor trustee(s) you select becomes the trustee(s). The successor trustee will have a fiduciary obligation to follow the terms of the trust. If maintaining your collection is important to you, you should select a trustee who has experience in managing collections or at least provide the trustee with specific guidance of who they should consult regarding the collection or what they should consider in maintaining the collection. If maintaining your collection intact for future generations, you should also consider how much liquidity, would be necessary to preserve the collection.

A revocable trust, in itself, does not result in specific tax savings. But the advantages are important: While the terms of a will can be public knowledge, the terms of a trust are private, and within the control of you and the parties that you select to be involved in the process. Assets will be transferred soon after death, legal fees can be minimized and the terms will remain private. Also, there may be less risk of an unhappy family member contesting a trust than a will.

Additionally, there may be ancillary tax benefits. The trust will provide for the disposition of your assets in accordance with your wishes. In addition, the trust will permit you to take full advantage of the marital estate tax deduction and your lifetime tax exemption by designating the exact proportion of assets to be distributed to specified recipients.

One of the other major benefits of a living trust is that it can contain directions for the trustee as to the care and protection of your assets, should you be unable to make such decisions due to your health or mental condition. Your designated trustee will assume control of your property and make the necessary decisions—which is a better option than putting a judge in control of your assets, which would occur without proper planning. Keep in mind, there are costs to consider associated with managing the trust. For example, if an art collection is owned by the trust, it might require storage, insurance, conservation, security, and other services associated with the ongoing care and management of the collection.

As an heir to a taxable estate, once the donor or owner of the collectible has passed away, most of your opportunities to reduce the estate tax consequences will have passed. It can be awkward, but if you're worried that a parent or anyone else from whom you are likely to inherit property has not been engaging the right advisors for estate planning, you should suggest a family meeting with their advisors to ensure all documents are in accordance with their wishes.

If it is necessary to liquidate all or part of the collection to pay estate taxes, the expenses of that liquidation (shipping, insurance, auction fees, commissions, etc.) are generally deductible from the estate. Additionally, estate expenses related to the use of lawyers and probate costs are deductible from the total gross estate. It is advantageous to arrange your estate plan to reduce these expenses rather than to deduct them (see living trust).

Mike Zeck and Others *Marvel Super-Heroes Secret Wars #8*
Story Page 25 Black Costume/Venom Original Art (Marvel, 1984).
Sold for $3,360,000 | January 2022

Nicolai Fechin (American, 1881-1955)
Taos Studio Interior
Oil on Canvas
20 x 24 inches
Sold for $237,500 | May 2023
Property from the Estate of Lois Brennand, Santa Fe, New Mexico

If you are the surviving spouse of the deceased, exemptions generally allow the estate to pass to you without taxes being owed. However, the estate planning burden then becomes yours, as the same marital tax exemptions will not apply at your death unless you remarry. If this eventuality was not already considered in your planning, you should contact an estate or tax professional without delay. Even if the survivor's estate issues were considered in the original planning, it cannot hurt to reevaluate the situation with a trusted advisor.

Life Insurance and Taxes

> "Helpful self-test questionnaire to see if you have enough life insurance (Sponsored by the Life Insurance Institute):
> 1.) How much life insurance do you have? ___
> 2.) You need more.
> 3.) We'll send somebody over right now." – Dave Barry

Although most of us have certain suspicions regarding insurance advisors, the truth is that life insurance is one of the most valuable tools available under our current tax structure. An expert insurance advisor is a critical component of your estate planning team. Ideally, long-term life insurance should be purchased while you are young and healthy. The same benefits may not be available should you become ill or incapacitated. Do not wait until you are in poor health, or when you are at such an age that the costs of insurance are prohibitive.

There are two primary purposes for life insurance in planning for estates substantial enough to incur taxation at the maximum rate.

The first is liquidity. In a proper plan, life insurance should be held outside of your estate. The IRS will want its money right away, and the liquidity provided by a life insurance payout may allow your heirs to avoid having to sell your collections at "fire sale" prices. Remember, not all insurance proceeds are excluded from your estate: If you are the owner of the policy or you name either yourself or your estate as the beneficiary, the proceeds will be included in the valuation of your estate upon death.

If the estate is structured properly, the tax burden falls primarily on the estate of the last spouse to die. As a result of the unlimited marital deduction and the maximum use of exemptions, the bulk of your estate can go to your spouse and vice-versa. To reduce the cost of the life insurance and to provide the liquidity for the estate taxes, it makes sense to insure the last to die.

Assuming that both spouses are alive, most advisors recommend that you purchase a whole life insurance policy on both spouses that will pay when the last spouse passes away. This is known as a "last to die" policy.

There is one more problem: Who should pay the premiums on the policy? The heirs are the likely source for the payment of the premiums.

Why? Because your heirs will be the beneficiaries of your generosity.

But how do they find the money to pay the premiums? Most collectors should use the annual gift tax exemption to give their heirs an amount that covers the cost of the premiums. Remember, you can make annual gifts of $19,000, or $38,000 if your spouse joins you. You essentially are purchasing a life insurance policy to benefit your heirs, while at the same time giving them cash gifts with which to pay the premiums. Life (insurance) is not always fair.

> **TIPS FOR HEIRS:** An ILIT is an important planning tool that provides liquidity to pay for any estate tax liabilities; the proceeds are not included in your estate. You may gift the premium amounts to your heirs using the annual gift tax exclusion; the insurance proceeds will be received tax-free by your heirs to be used to pay the estate taxes. It is important to make sure that the documents are drafted properly by an expert and the gifts are made in accordance with IRS rulings. Insurance is a critical strategy for any substantial estate — make an expert a part of your team.

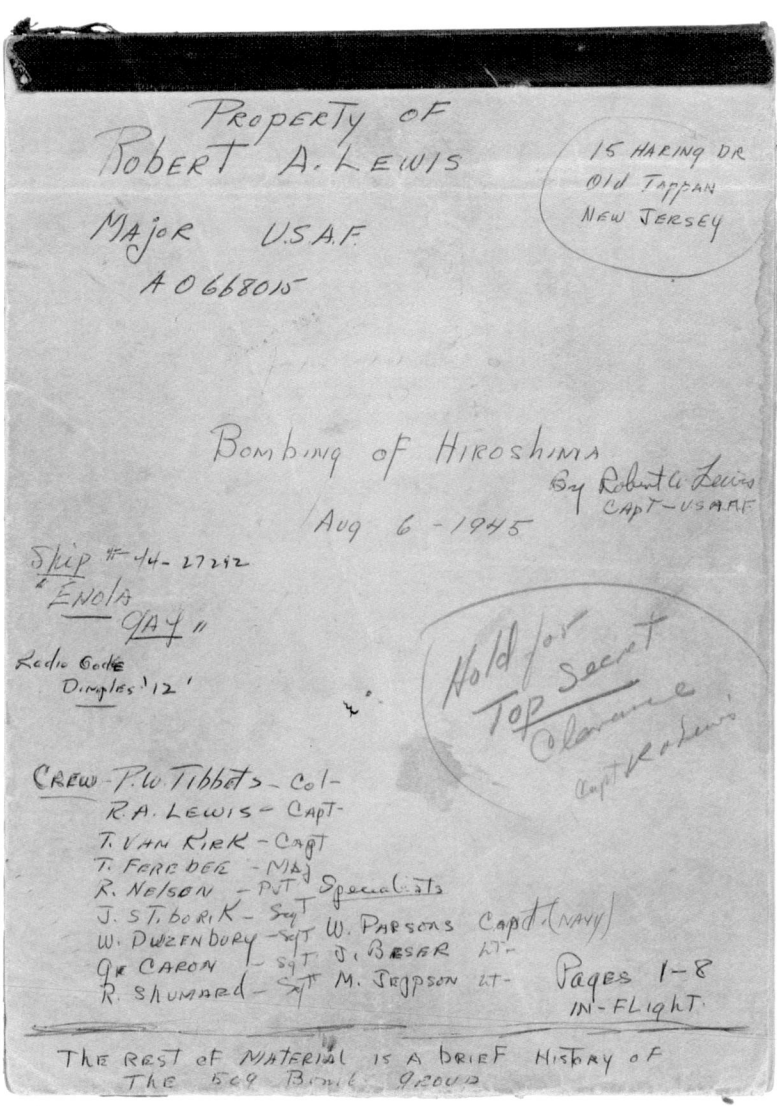

[World War II, Bombing of Hiroshima]. Autograph Logbook of Capt. Robert A. Lewis [USAAF, Co-Pilot of the Enola Gay], containing the only IN-FLIGHT account of the "Little Boy" mission and the bombing of Hiroshima, Japan. August 6, 1945
Sold for $543,000 | July 2022

Kathleen Guzman's Story ....

Kathleen Guzman is a former managing director at Heritage Auctions, having joined the firm in 2006 after a career that included serving as President of Christie's East and President of Phillips Auctioneers and as Senior Vice President of Business Development at eBay. She has appeared as an antiques expert on Oprah, Good Morning America, and CNN, and is probably best recognized for having served as an appraiser on Antiques Roadshow for more than 20 years.

Sometimes the business of treasure hunting and treasure dealing has a way of imitating the stories behind the objects collectors covet. The best example of this phenomenon in my career came in 1994, when I orchestrated the sale of the original Maltese Falcon.

In the 1941 movie classic The Maltese Falcon — based on the 1931 Dashiell Hammett novel of the same name — Casper Gutman (played by Sydney Greenstreet) offers private investigator Sam Spade (Humphrey Bogart) $25,000 plus a quarter of the sale proceeds for help locating a figurine of a black bird believed to be filled with priceless jewels.

In 1994 — by which time the film was widely considered the first example of film noir and recently had been added to the Library of Congress' National Film Registry — I was the president of Christie's East, and a lady named Tippy Stringer called our Beverly Hills office about a few items she was looking to sell, so I headed out to have a look.

Stringer was one of the first female weather reporters and a television legend in her own right, but the marquee lot of her collection came from her late husband, the actor William Conrad. Sitting on the shelf in Stringer's library — in the background, propping up a row of leather-bound books — was the original Maltese Falcon used in the movie, a gift to Conrad from Warner Brothers studio head Jack Warner.

The Maltese Falcon, an elusive object in the movie, also is an elusive object in real life, and the object at which I was looking had been presumed lost for decades. The Warner Brothers Archives cite two examples produced for the film, which the stagehands remember using for weight-lifting competitions; they weighed 45 pounds each, and one of them was in the collection of a California dentist. During the filming of the movie, the statue fell from actress Lee Patrick's hands and landed on Bogart's left foot, causing a minor injury. Seeing it on the shelf, then taking it down to examine it and noticing the Warner Brothers prop house number, my hands trembled.

The Maltese Falcon — the highlight of the film and television memorabilia sale — was up for auction Dec. 6, 1994, and I was the auctioneer in a sale that also included Academy Awards for Gone With the Wind and a copy of that book signed by the cast of the movie.

The pre-sale estimate for the Maltese Falcon was $30,000-$50,000, but intense interest at the viewing and a few absentee bids had driven our internal estimate up to $150,000. Film noir buffs had traveled far to see the prop — some came dressed as Humphrey Bogart, hoping to take a picture with it, and one lady came looking to measure it for the design of the table she was planning to build for it. That kind of interest is every seller's dream, but also created the potential for an unhappy experience for auction-goers. Our inadvertently low estimate had brought out more than a few people who thought they would have a shot at the Falcon for a fraction of what we knew by then knew it would bring.

I instantly knew what to do: I wanted to lighten the atmosphere in the room and give every auction-goer a chance to at least bid on it, so I started the bidding at $1. Every hand in the room shot up, and the place roared with laughter. The people in attendance got the memory of their lives and they were able to tell their families and friends that they bid on the Maltese Falcon!

When the hammer came down, the Maltese Falcon sold for $398,500, a record price at the time for a film prop, and also surely a record price for a lead bird with a bronze patina! The buyer was Ronald Winston, president of the New York-based Harry Winston jewelry chain — but before he could be identified by the press gathered there, Winston fled the room. The newscasts that night showed the flight of the mysterious buyer of the Maltese Falcon. When Winston formally announced his acquisition, there were high hopes, based on the family's past generosity, that the piece ended up in the Smithsonian. But it was not meant to be: the Maltese Falcon reportedly was sold to a reclusive sheikh for more than $1 million, and the elusive bird has not been seen since.

The Estate of
Kenneth Alan Hill, Sr.

Fort Worth, Texas

Kenneth Alan Hill, Sr., turned his love of the water into a lifetime of collecting. The Fort Worth, Texas, resident and retired pharmaceutical pioneer sought only the finest examples of maritime fine art and antiques to complete a truly outstanding collection. "Hill's astute collector's eye pursued objects rarely seen outside of institutions," said Michelle Castro, Vice President of Trusts & Estates at Heritage Auctions. "His taste was impeccable and now his collection is ready for an entirely new generation of connoisseurs."

Versace Dinner Service
A Two Hundred-Two Piece Versace Les Trésors De La Mer Pattern Porcelain Dinner Service for Twelve, June 2021
Sold for $37,500

A Carved Bone Napoleonic
Prisoner-of-War Ship HMS
Alexander Model, circa 1795-1815
May 2021
Sold for $62,500

Montague Dawson (British, 1895-1973)
Night suspect, 1958, June 2021
OIl on Canvas
40 x 50 inches
Sold for $175,000

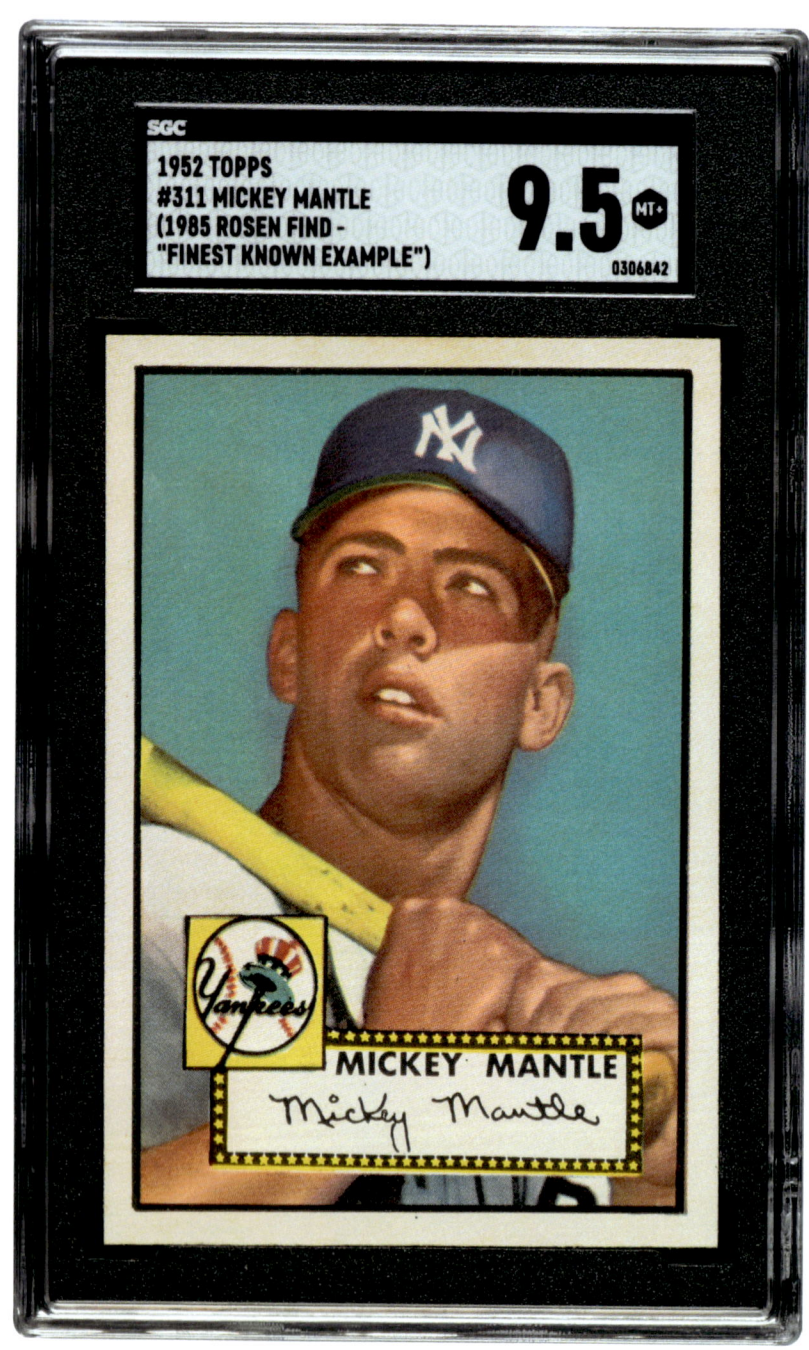

1952 Topps Mickey Mantle #311 SGC Mint+ 9.5 - 1985 Rosen Find -
"Finest Known Example!"
Sold for $12,600,000 | August 2022

8

Collectibles and Charitable Giving

"In faith and hope the world will disagree, but all mankind's concern is charity." – Alexander The Great

"To give requires good sense." – Ovid

Americans gave $592.5 billion to charity in 2024, and individual donors contributed close to 64 percent of that amount; in total, charitable giving represents about 2 percent of GDP.

Collectors consider philanthropic giving because they want to support a specific charity or make a positive impact on their community. In addition, charitable giving provides donors the opportunity to obtain a charitable deduction for income, gift or estate taxes. There are many factors to consider with charitable giving in order to optimize your tax benefits.

Charitable Giving Nuts and Bolts

For those that are charitably inclined, gifts can be made using cash or property, both real estate and tangible personal property which include collectibles. When making gifts to charities other than by cash the amount of your ability to deduct the gift may be limited. If tax savings is your primary goal in making a charitable gift it is imperative that you involve your tax planner, attorney and financial advisor, because the rules are complicated. If your collection has appreciated, whether you can deduct the full fair market value of the gift or be limited to your cost basis will depend on specified criteria. . Here is what it takes to qualify:

1. The donated items are qualified capital gains property

This generally means that the donated items have been in the collection for at least a year, are not tangible items created by you (because if they were, you would only be allowed to deduct the cost of materials in most cases), and were not gifted to you by their creator.

Complete Collection of Signers of the Declaration of Independence.
Sold for $1,395,000 | June 2022

2. The donee organization is a qualified public charity

Public charities generally receive at least part of their support from the public. IRS Section 501(c)(3) lists the types of donee organizations and the guidelines for them to follow to qualify for the charitable deduction. The charity must serve a public interest and must meet an "organizational test." Additionally, the organization must be organized and operated for a religious, charitable, scientific, literary or educational purpose.

Churches, schools and museums are generally considered to be qualified public charities, while private foundations are not. The difference is that you receive a deduction based only upon the actual cost of the donated item when you give to a private foundation, while a public charitable donation can be deducted at full fair market value. It is reasonable for a potential donor to request that an organization write a letter confirming that the IRS has made a determination that the organization qualifies for tax-exempt status under Section 501(c)(3), and that the charity intends to use the objects for a valid charitable purpose.

3. The donee organization must make "related use" of the donation

Your gift of tangible personal property must relate to the exempt purposes or functions of the organization. For example, if you donate a coin collection to the American Numismatic Society for the purpose of expanding its museum collections, you would receive a deduction of fair market value since the collection relates to the Society's mission of increasing the knowledge and enjoyment of coin collecting.

If you donate the coins to a hospital that intends to sell the collection and use the revenue for its capital campaign, you can only deduct your cost of acquisition. The difference between types of use is subjective and often confusing, so it is important to determine the use for the gift. Make sure that the qualified organization actually wants the donation. The organization should provide a written acceptance of the collection or item, stating that it is a qualified public charity and that the donation satisfies the related use rule.

An additional factor, which reinforces the importance of communicating with the charity, is that a charitable deduction for contributions of tangible personal property exceeding $5,000 must be reduced or recaptured if the donee sells the property for less than your deducted amount within three years of the contribution.

4. The collection has a "qualified appraisal"

The IRS requires a qualified appraisal if the gift of property is more than $5,000. If the gift is greater than $20,000, a complete copy of the signed appraisal must be attached to the tax return.

A qualified appraiser is an individual who holds himself out to the public as an appraiser and has earned an appraisal designation from a recognized professional organization or has otherwise met certain education and experience requirements, regularly performs appraisals for compensation, and meets any other IRS requirements.

Other Issues in Charitable Giving

Most charities know very little about collectible assets. If you want your donation to be a meaningful contribution, you have to determine how the charity will use your collection.

In most cases, that means that it will have to sell your collection to raise funds. Unless you are donating the collection to a museum that will display it or use it for research, it might be best to sell it and donate the proceeds to your charity. If you choose not to sell your collection during your lifetime, then you should leave detailed written instructions for the disposition of your gift.

If your selected charity can not accept your donation and would prefer to monetize it, selling it at auction is a good alternative. Make sure you select an auctioneer with experience selling your collecting category. The charity of choice can be named as beneficiary of the proceeds from the auction. Assisting the charity in planning for the sale of your collection ensures that the charity will receive the maximum return without exhausting its own resources.

Magic: The Gathering Artist Proof Black Lotus Limited Edition (Beta)
CGC Trading Card Game NM/Mint+ 8.5 (Wizards of the Coast, 1993)
Signed by Christopher Rush
Sold for $610,000 | March 2023

Limitations and the Five-Year Carryover

What if you donate an item of considerable value that results in a very large tax deduction relative to your income level?

The IRS limits the amount of a charitable income tax deduction to a percentage of current income. If the donation is made to a qualified public charity, and the gift is considered a related use, you can deduct the current fair market value up to 30 percent of your adjusted gross income. If the donation is made to a qualified public charity, but is a non-related use, then your deduction is limited to your cost basis up to 50 percent of your adjusted gross income. However, you can carry forward the excess deductions for up to five years, until the amount is fully deducted.

For example, a collector with an adjusted gross income of $100,000 has a coin that he purchased for $50,000 in 1985; it is now worth $150,000. The collector donates it to a museum that plans to exhibit it. Because the donation is to a qualifying organization and is a related use, he can deduct the fair market value of $150,000, subject to a limit of 30 percent of his current adjusted gross income. Therefore, in the current year he is able to deduct $30,000 and can carry forward the remaining $120,000 in deductions over the next four years.

Donating a Fractional Interest

Fractional giving is a process where you donate percentages of ownership of a collection or single object over a multi-year time frame. The percentage that you donate is the percentage that you can receive as a charitable tax deduction. Historically, it benefited public institutions while it allowed the donors both estate and capital gains tax deductions. It provided the added benefit of allowing the donor to retain possession for a period of time, and the affiliation of the collection with the museum has the potential to increase the collection's value (and increase the charitable tax deduction).

The Pension Protection Act of 2006 directs donors to gift the entire interest in the collection to the charity within 10 years of the initial donation, or death, whichever comes first. Also, the donee institution must maintain substantial physical possession of the object within 10 years of the initial contribution. Since the laws involving fractional giving remain in a state of flux, fractional gifts may be a very difficult estate planning option. Collectors who are considering making fractional gifts should obtain expert advice prior to gifting.

Charitable Remainder Trusts

A charitable remainder trust (CRT) is beneficial if you want both income and a tax deduction, and are prepared to give up your collection now.

It is particularly advantageous if the collection has enjoyed significant appreciation since the time of acquisition, and you are no longer emotionally attached to it. In this arrangement, the donation is made to the qualifying charity in trust. The charity agrees to pay you annually, either through a fixed amount of money (annuity trust) or a percentage of the trust's total value (unitrust) for life, or for a set number of years (not to exceed 20).

The benefit is that if you sold the collection yourself to create income, the principal amount would be reduced by the taxes on the capital gains (28 percent). In a CRT, the trustee can sell the collection tax free and create a larger principal base. You can claim the collection's future or remainder value (based on IRS tables) as a charitable deduction in the year that the property is transferred to the trust because the trust is considered a "non-related use." You receive your agreed-upon payments, and when the trust period is complete, all remaining interest in the trust passes to the charity with both you and the institution avoiding capital gains taxes on the appreciated value of the items. Ultimately, you receive a regular income stream, while avoiding estate taxes and probate by transferring the asset out of the estate.

There are some caveats. Most collectibles are not "income producing assets," so the collection — at least most of it — may have to be sold within the first year of the trust in order to fund it with qualifying financial vehicles. The annual distribution to the donor must be a minimum of 5 percent of the trust's value and a maximum of 50 percent. Additionally, at the conclusion of the agreement, the remainder to the qualified charity must be at least 10 percent of the initial value. These rules are subject to change, and create a certain amount of latitude in the trust agreement that must be negotiated between the donor and the charity.

A charitable remainder trust is a gift that keeps on giving. This may be one of the few gifts that you ever receive from the IRS. Where else in the Internal Revenue Code are you able to make a charitable donation, receive an immediate tax deduction that may be carried forward if necessary, and reduce your estate and potential estate tax while you receive an income for a period of years without paying?

Other Trust Variations

Trusts are complex legal documents that must be drafted properly or you may lose all of the potential tax benefits. An expert is required to avoid future complications. The trusts referred to in this section are irrevocable and once property is transferred, only a few minor changes are permitted without harmful results. At the time you transfer your collectibles to the trust, you will be entitled to an immediate income tax deduction. Retain a qualified appraiser who is familiar with the IRS rules, to prepare an appraisal to support the value of the property.

The IRS, as we have and will discuss, has strict rules regarding the qualifications for a qualified appraiser and appraisal. The amount of the deduction is the fair market (not the actual cost) value of the assets discounted over the length of the trust assuming you have owned these objects for more than one year.

The length of the trust may be term certain (not to exceed 20 years) or it may continue over the term of your life, or the lives of you and your spouse. The longer the term of the trust, the less the charitable deduction, but the longer you will receive a stream of income. As stated above, the benefits of these types or trusts is more the ability to receive a stream of income based on fair market value of the contributed asset(s) as opposed to maximizing the charitable deduction from your gift.

The amount of the immediate deduction may offset only 30 percent of your adjusted gross income in the first year; however, if the deduction cannot be fully used in the first year, it may be carried forward for up to five years. The trust is tax exempt and is able to sell appreciated assets without incurring any capital gains. This means that the full sale proceeds (not just the after-tax portion) can be invested to generate an annual income for life for you and/or your spouse.

Here is what this means: if you sold your collection today for $3 million, and you paid $1 million for it 10 years ago, you would likely pay the 28 percent capital gains tax, which would leave you with a $560,000 tax bill.

The net amount available for investment would be $2.44 million ($3 million, minus the $560,000 tax) that you could invest as you may determine. However, the trust will be able to invest the entire $3 million and provide you with an income for life, or lives, or up to 20 years at a

Edward VIII Gold Proof Pattern 5 Pounds 1937
PR67 Ultra Cameo NGC
Sold for $2,280,000 | March 2021
From the Paramount Collection

rate that the donor (you) determines with the charity. The asset is now out of your estate and no longer subject to estate taxes.

The only other rules are that the annual distributions from the trust must be a minimum of 5 percent of the value, and a maximum of 50 percent. Also, when the trust ends, the remainder that goes to the charity must be at least 10 percent of the initial value of the contribution.

This is the ideal solution for anyone whose collection has appreciated significantly in value, who would like to sell the collection and does not have heirs interested in owning the collectibles.

The other, less favorable, alternative is to retain the collection until you die, at which point your heirs will receive a stepped-up basis if they sell the assets. The assets, though, will be included in the value of the estate, which may in itself create a tax if exemptions do not preclude estate taxation at the time of death.

André Brasilier (b. 1929)
Chevaux au crépuscule irlandais, 1983
Oil on Canvas
38 x 57 inches
Sold for $106,250 | November 2022
Property from a Distinguished Estate, Newport Beach, California

Helpful Tips on Non-Cash Charitable Contributions

• Speak with a tax advisor prior to considering a non-cash charitable contribution. It may be in the donor's best interest to sell the property and donate the cash.

• A Qualified Appraisal Report written by a Qualified Appraiser is required when the fair market value of the donated item exceeds $5,000.

• Appraisals cannot be made more than 60 days prior to the date of donation, but they can be made any time after the donation is made up until the taxpayer's return is due.

• IRS Form 8283 is required for all non-cash charitable gifts and when a gift exceed $5,000 in value, the form must be completed by the donor and then signed by both the appraiser and the donee. The donee is also required to provide the donor with contemporaneous written acknowledgement.

TIPS FOR HEIRS: In summary, when it comes to charitable planning and your collection, there are many options available to you, each with benefits and pitfalls. When considering making a charitable gift, it is extremely important that you collaborate with your advisory team and the charitable institution to ensure that your gift will provide both you and the organization with the maximum benefits.

Nobel Auction for Ukraine Brings $103.5 Million

Russian Journalist Dmitry Muratov Sells Nobel Peace Prize Medal To Benefit Displaced Ukrainian Children

By Robert Wilonsky

The 2021 Nobel Peace Prize medal awarded to independent Russian journalist and *Novaya Gazeta* editor-in-chief Dmitry Muratov fetched $103.5 million from an anonymous Heritage Auctions bidder at a live global auction at the Times Center in Manhattan on June 20.

Proceeds raised from the auction went directly to support UNICEF's humanitarian response to the war in Ukraine and affected regions. Heritage Auctions donated its efforts to bring worldwide attention to Muratov's desire to aid those impacted by the war.

"Several months ago, we at *Novaya Gazeta* asked ourselves what we could do to stop the war and help these civilians get their lives back,"

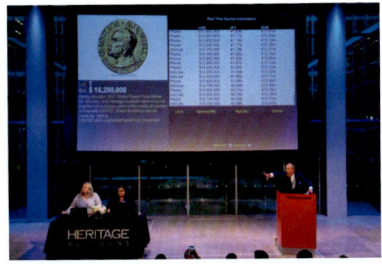

Muratov said during the June 20 event. "We decided to sell our Nobel Peace Prize medal through Heritage Auctions, which managed the process very efficiently and waived all their fees and commissions completely. We thank them for this."

Bidding on the medal opened June 1, Children's Day in Ukraine, and concluded June 20, World Refugee Day, commemorating the strength, courage and perseverance of refugees.

The medal opened live bidding at $787,500, then quickly reached $1 million; then, $2 million; then, $3 million. And each time bids reached a round number, the auditorium burst into applause. Bidders over the phone and on HA.com eventually drove the price past $16 million. Then, about 23 minutes after the auction began, one phone bidder moved to the front of the line with a bid of $103.5 million. The room erupted.

"UNICEF is honored, excited and deeply grateful to Dmitry Muratov for his extraordinary generosity, and we are astounded by the unprecedented response to the auction," says UNICEF Executive Director Catherine Russell. "This remarkable contribution will help Ukrainian children survive this brutal war and, someday, rebuild their lives. We hope Mr. Muratov's gift inspires others to support vulnerable children in Ukraine and everywhere. We also want to thank the anonymous bidder, whose winning bid will do so much for so many."

Buddy Holly & the Crickets
"The Day the Music Died"
1959 Historic Concert Poster
Sold for $447,000 | November 2022

PART THREE

Evaluating Your Collection

1870-S $3 SP50 -- 893 Engraved
PCGS. Unique
Sold for $5,520,000 | January 2023

9

:::

Third-Party Authentication
and Grading

Authenticity and evaluation are vital matters for any collection. This chapter concentrates on third-party grading services that are available to grade and authenticate your collectibles. These services are widely available for coins, sports cards and comics. Use them as needed, but consider the cost, quality and value of grading services for your collectibles. For many items, especially lesser-valued pieces, grading may not be necessary.

For coin grading, the American Numismatic Association (ANA) adopted Dr. William Sheldon's 70-point grading system and, between 1973 and 1977, worked to establish standards for all series under the leadership of numismatic luminary Abe Kosoff. Experts from all coin specialties collaborated with Kosoff to develop the first official ANA grading guide, published in 1978.

Initially, it recognized three grades to evaluate Mint State coins: Uncirculated or MS-60; Choice Uncirculated or MS-65; and Perfect Uncirculated or MS-70. Unfortunately, the third grade (MS-70) was mostly theoretical, and the two remaining designations quickly proved inadequate for the marketplace. MS-63 (Select Uncirculated) and MS-67 (Gem Uncirculated) were added to the system and functioned successfully for a while until the demand for closer evaluation required additional grades. Eventually, all numbers between MS-60 and MS-70 were employed and the adjectival equivalents were eliminated.

NGC and PCGS remain the acknowledged leaders for coin grading. The reason for their success is that they are the only firms that have maintained sufficient dealer confidence to allow coins to be traded routinely on a sight-unseen basis.

Comics and cards are generally graded on a 10-point scale, with a "10" being the highest grade (most perfect quality). Several grading services are listed for these collectible categories in the Appendix. For comics, Comics Guaranty, LLC (CGC) is recognized as the most trusted grading service.

Sports card authenticity is often entrusted to one of three major grading houses: Professional Sports Authenticator (PSA), Beckett Grading Services (BGS) and Sportscard Guaranty LLC (SGC). Talk to your local card dealers, or find one online and ask which grading service has the most credibility among dealers and collectors. Collectors' with autographed items use PSA/DNA to authenticate their collectibles. They also are listed in the Appendix to this book.

Stamp collectors frequently rely on the grading services of Professional Stamp Experts (PSE). The PSE website (see Appendix) contains detailed instructions and an online submission kit, each of which is an excellent guide on how to properly submit stamps for grading.

What Should You Certify?

Certification is an expensive proposition that should be approached with caution. At $15 and up per item, the total costs — for even a small collection — easily can run into the thousands of dollars. Not all collectibles benefit equally from being certified. The rule of thumb, of course, is that the finished product has to be worth more than the raw (ungraded) item, plus the certification fee.

There are two practical reasons to certify a collectible: to determine authenticity and to add value.

When a dealer considers buying an uncertified collectible, the guess is how the grading service is going to grade it — and the dealer will want to be as conservative as possible. For example, if a dealer is looking at your 1886-O Morgan dollar and is trying to decide whether NGC will grade it an MS-63 (valued at, say, $3,000) or MS-64 (valued at $10,000), it will be designated as an MS-63 coin, to be on the safe side, and offer a price commensurate with an MS-63 coin.

Alaska Centennial Gold Nugget
Sold for $750,000 | December 2021

You could, however, have the coin certified before attempting to sell it. The upside is that if the grading service calls it an MS-64, you have a five-figure coin. The downside is the cost of the grading fee. The bottom line is that this issue has a significant value spread between grades and — in our opinion — the risk is worth the expense.

Submitting Your Coins

NGC and PCGS both operate primarily through authorized dealer networks, though both offer programs through which collectors can directly submit coins to the grading services. Most of these dealers frequently will submit your coins to the grading services on your behalf. The dealer often is compensated with a rebate of approximately 20 percent of the grading fee. Don't request part of the rebate, but do ask for the coins to be previewed and for help determining which coins to submit for certification. Most authorized dealers are familiar with the standards of both grading services and can help you avoid coin submissions on which third-party grading may not add value.

If you reside within driving distance of an authorized dealer, make an appointment to preview the coins with them. If you are not within a reasonable distance, you may ship your coins to an authorized dealer of your choice. A good rule of thumb is to select an authorized dealer who is also a member of the Professional Numismatists Guild (PNG). The PNG is the most respected numismatic fraternal organization and each new candidate must undergo a detailed background check and be approved by the entire membership. Members must conduct themselves under a strict Code of Ethics and submit to binding arbitration in the event of disputes. Contact information for the PNG is also included in the Appendix A.

Declaring Submission Value for Insurance

When you prepare to submit your collectibles for grading, you will be asked to declare a value for insurance purposes. This is important should the package become lost or the items damaged in transit or at the grading service. Since grading and shipping fees both are impacted by this decision, you need to determine whether the value range is commensurate with the likelihood of loss or damage, and then select a replacement value for the items. Third-party grading can be an extremely important part of estate planning. Certification by a reputable grading system will increase the liquidity of a collection when it is sold because certified coins are easy to trade among dealers and on the Internet. Your heirs and advisors will be spared the burden of extensive (and expensive) identification and cataloging.

Third-party grading will protect your collectibles, allow your heirs to value and identify them, and provide liquidity when the collection is sold.

TIPS FOR HEIRS: As a non-collector, submitting items for third-party grading and authentication for the important items in your inheritance will provide you and your heirs with a far greater comfort level in assessing the real value of the collection. Because you are probably unfamiliar with the language and nuances of the hobby, we recommend that you devote additional time to qualifying the authorized dealer you consult. Speak plainly about your goals and ask a lot of questions. If you are not satisfied with the responses to your questions, don't hesitate to request a more detailed explanation. You can never know too much about your inheritance, but knowing too little can be extremely dangerous.

Louis Vuitton SS21 Virgil Abloh Malle Courrier Lozine 110 Steamer Trunk
Sold for $87,500 | May 2022

1970's Muhammad Ali WBC Heavyweight
Championship Belt Earned in Victory over
George Foreman in the "Rumble in the Jungle."
Sold for $6,180,000 | July 2022

10

Having Your Collection Appraised

The appraisal of tangible personal property is an integral part of estate and financial planning and collection management. Included here are some frequently asked questions and tips.

APPRAISAL FAQS

Do I need an Appraisal?
You may need an appraisal for a variety of purposes including:
- Gaining and maintaining accurate insurance coverage for your property
- Evaluating federal estate tax liability in cases of death
- Evaluating federal gift tax liability
- Reporting non-cash charitable contributions to the IRS
- Assisting with estate and financial planning
- Equitably dividing assets in an estate
- Equitably dividing assets in a divorce proceeding
- Setting a valuation basis for a collateral loan

What is the difference between an appraisal and auction estimate? An appraisal report requires adherence to USPAP guidelines, IRS regulations, and liability agreements. Appraisals set a specific value for a specific purpose at a specific time — such as a fair market value appraisal for estate tax purposes as of the date of death or a replacement value appraisal for insurance purposes as of today's market. Appraisals are a fee-based service, with the cost factoring in the amount of research involved to pinpoint a specific value that will often be used by a third party to establish a basis for insurance coverage, tax liability, or a collateral for a loan.

Auction estimates are quick and free opinions of the current market value of items. The intent is to provide the owner of an asset with an understanding of how much might be realized in the current market through a sale at auction. While the intent is to provide rough guidance as to value, such estimates are not intended for establishing a value for insurance, tax, estate planning, collateral, third-party transactions or other purposes.

How do I choose a qualified appraiser?

When hiring an appraiser, it is good practice to choose one that is USPAP-compliant. A USPAP-compliant appraiser will have been trained and tested in appraisal methodology, ethical standards, and advanced report-writing skills. Continuing education is also required for appraisers to maintain and grow their market knowledge and expertise.

Select an appraiser who has formal education and longtime experience in the type of property being appraised.

What is USPAP?

USPAP is the acronym for the Uniform Standards of Professional Appraisal Practice issued by The Appraisal Foundation and updated periodically. They are the generally accepted standards for professional appraisal practice in North America for all appraisal disciplines, including real property, personal property, business valuation, and mass appraisal.

Are there different types of values?

The short answer is yes. The two main concepts of value are fair market value and retail replacement value (or replacement cost). The starting place for determining value used by appraisers is the definition of fair market value found in Treasury regulations, which are the official clarification of the internal revenue code promulgated by the Department of Treasury.

Treasury Regulation §20.2031-1(b) defines fair market value as "the price at which the property would change hands between a willing buyer and a willing seller, neither being under any compulsion to buy or to sell and both having reasonable knowledge of relevant facts. The fair market value of a particular item of property includible in the decedent's gross estate is not to be determined by a forced sale price. Nor is the fair market value of an item of property to be determined by the sale price of the item in a market other than that in which such item is most commonly sold to the public, taking into account the location of the item wherever appropriate." Fair market value is used by the IRS when evaluating transfers between parties during life through gifts to friends, family or charities or in a sale (a sale for less than fair market value could be deemed part gift, part sale), when securing a loan (collateral) or death for determine estate tax liability for equitable division of assets.

Replacement cost, on the other hand, may begin with "fair market value" but also takes into account other factors such as expenses that would be incurred to replace an item which might include shipping, handling, commissions, taxes and other acquisition costs, When insuring an item that you want to maintain and reacquire if it is lost, stolen or damaged

Neil Armstrong's One and Only Apollo 11 Lunar Module
Flown MS67 NGC 14K Gold Robbins Medal Directly From
The Armstrong Family Collection™, CAG Certified.
Sold for $2,055,000 | July 2019

Bob Dylan 1963 Original *Freewheelin'* Album
w/Four Deleted Tracks
In Super-Rare Stereo.
Sold for $150,000 | July 2022

beyond repair, you should insure based on replacement cost of the insured item because your out of pocket cost to replace the item will undoubtedly exceed the "fair market value."

Even though the concepts may seem simple and straightforward, there are still many nuances that get factored when trying to determine the appropriate value. As such, using the right appraiser is of utmost importance. Moreover, on July 30, 2018, the IRS announced final regulations that define who is a Qualified Appraiser and what is considered a Qualified Appraisal. It is now more important than ever to ensure you are hiring a knowledgeable appraiser who has both education and experience with the items being appraised and understands how to produce a credible appraisal report.

Replacement value is defined as the amount it would cost to replace an item with one similar and like quality purchased in the most appropriate marketplace within a reasonable amount of time. Replacement value often includes not only the costs of acquiring or replicating the property, but also all the relevant costs associated with replacement. These other costs may include all applicable taxes and duties, framing, crating and transportation.

How often should I update my insurance appraisal?
Check with your insurance company first for their guidelines and recommendations for appraisal updates, but generally, we recommend that insurance appraisals be updated every one to five years depending on the type of property you collect to keep informed with the most current market valuations.

How do I prepare for an appraisal, and what should I expect?
Ensure that all items being appraised are easily accessible, create a preliminary inventory of your items, and/or take detailed photographs of your collections. These preliminary inventories and photographs may also help us advise you on whether an appraisal is necessary.

Having an inventory of your collection is good collection management practice. Update the inventory as you add to or subtract from your collection. Many collection management software programs are available to the public. Provenance, receipts, and good photos not only assist with the appraisal process but protect your family history by compiling stories of how your collection was acquired to pass on your collection's legacy to future generations.

An appraiser may be able to determine the scope of the appraisal from preliminary information and images provided by the client. However, in some cases, an initial on-site evaluation may be necessary for the appraiser to determine the scope of work.

A qualified appraiser should have the appraisal terms and conditions outlined in an appraisal agreement, including the estimated fee for the appraisal.

Appraisers charge an hourly or daily rate, or a negotiated flat rate based on time or the number of items. An appraiser's fee should not be calculated based on a percentage of the value of the property.

Certain types of personal property may require grading or authentication by outside experts. Appraisers are not authenticators or graders, and appraisal reports are not proof of authenticity. However, appraisers can often assist with grading and authentication services as letters or certificates of authenticity can be obtained from the recognized authority in each art and collectible field.

After the inspection, either by photograph or personal examination, and after research has been concluded, appraisers will produce a written report of their value opinions and conclusions.

Helpful Tips on Non-Cash Charitable Contributions
- Speak with a tax advisor prior to considering a non-cash charitable contribution. It may be in the donor's best interest to sell the property and donate the cash, rather than proceed with appraising property in accordance with IRS regulations.
- A Qualified Appraisal Report written by a Qualified Appraiser is required when the fair market value of the donated item exceeds $5,000.
- Appraisals cannot be made more than 60 days prior to the date of donation; but they can be made any time after the donation is made up until the taxpayer's return is due.
- IRS Form 8283 must be completed by the donor and then signed by both the appraiser and the donee. The donee is also required to provide the donor with contemporaneous written acknowledgement.
- On July 30, 2018, the IRS announced final regulations that define who is a Qualified Appraiser and what is considered a Qualified Appraisal. It is now more important than ever to ensure you are hiring a knowledgeable appraiser who has both education and experience with the items being appraised and understands how to produce a credible appraisal report.

A Massive Japanese Silver
Incense Burner, Meiji Period
Sold for $250,000 | May 2023

Greg Rohan's Story............

At the age of 8, Greg Rohan started collecting coins, and by 1971, at the age of 10, he was buying and selling coins from a dealer's table at trade shows in his hometown of Seattle. Today, as a partner and President of Heritage Auctions, his responsibilities include overseeing the firm's private client group and working with top collectors in every field in which Heritage Auctions is active.

Sometimes outstanding auction results are the product of a brilliant marketing strategy and the excitement generated by a once-in-a-lifetime opportunity to own something spectacular.

Sometimes. But just as often, pre-sale estimates are blown away by a confluence of coincidences — motives that have little to do with an item being exceptional, and end with a collector paying far more than an item would sell for on any other day. My favorite example of this phenomenon came on August 7, 2000, when we sold a 1919 Denver mint dime from the collection of a New Jersey State Senator named Lou Bassano. Bassano was a devoted collector in his late 50s and, at the urging of his wife, was selling off part of his coin collection to diversify his assets. The 1919 dime was in beautiful condition — the book value was around $30,000 but given its scarcity, we thought it could sell for perhaps $50,000.

By the time the auction started, Internet bidding had driven it up to $60,000, and Sen. Bassano and his wife were at the sale, looking quite pleased. Then the floor bidding started. It quickly climbed past $100,000, at which point there were two bidders left: a well-known collector sitting in the back with his wife, and a well-known dealer sitting in the front row, bidding on behalf of a collector with a discrete wave of his pen in order to preserve anonymity.

But I noticed something funny about the bidder in the back of the room: his wife was doing the bidding. Normally, he did the bidding, but this time he was arguing with his wife who was gleefully waving her paddle, keeping the auction going. I was puzzled. Did his wife even collect coins? What was going on?

By the time the bidding ended, the dealer in the front row was the winner at $218,500. The room broke into applause and I walked over to the couple in the back to console them on their defeat and thank them for driving up the price. The man was relieved: "Thank God we didn't get that," he said. "She's crazy." His wife explained that it was his birthday, and that it was the last coin he needed to complete a set, so she'd bid as high as he would let her, ignoring his pleas that it wasn't worth that much.

The next day I went over to see the dealer to deliver his purchase and collect a check. "You were quite the star," I told him.

"I've got a huge problem," he said. "How on earth could that sell for $218,500?"

"Well clearly it did," I replied. He explained that he'd purchased it on behalf of a client who hadn't bothered giving him a limit. He'd been told to buy the coin that was expected to sell in the $30,000-$50,000 range, totally unaware that the bidding would carry it to more than four times the high estimate.

"He told me to just buy the coin," he said nervously. "But I can just hear him saying 'I told you to buy the coin, not take a leave of your senses.' I don't know what to do."

"Well the first thing you need to do is write me a check," I said. "I'll put it in my desk while you go talk to your client and if he gives you trouble and you need more time to pay, I can wait awhile to cash it."

Everything worked out fine in the end. The collector was, of course, shocked to hear that he'd paid that much for it, but he honored his commitment. I think that Sen. Bassano probably got in more than a few "I told you so's" on the ride back to New Jersey with his wife, who had told him that she didn't think coins were a good investment.

The Estate of
Myra Janco Daniels
Naples, Florida

Heritage was thrilled to present selections from the Estate of Myra Janco Daniels across our Spring 2023 sales. Daniels was the arts visionary and advertising pioneer who helped transform Southwest Florida into a nationally recognized cultural destination. Daniels was the founder and CEO of the Philharmonic Center for the Arts (now Artis-Naples). While the arts were a lifelong passion, her first career was as a groundbreaking advertising executive in Chicago, where she was among the first women to head a national ad firm. Her husband, Draper Daniels, was responsible for many famous ad campaigns, including the Marlboro Man, and was later an inspiration for the Don Draper character on the popular TV series *Mad Men*.

Daum Blown-Out Glass Vase with Louis Majorelle Iron Mount, circa 1920
12 inches
Sold for $14,375

Opposite top:
Helen Frankenthaler
Beginnings, 2002
Screenprint in colors on handmade paper
37 x 36 inches
Sold for $30,000

Opposite bottom:
Wolf Kahn
A Dip in the Horizon, 1990
Oil on Canvas
26 x 28 inches
Sold for $42,500

125

Patek Philippe Very Rare And Important Ref. 3974J
Yellow Gold Automatic Perpetual Calendar Minute Repeating
Wristwatch With Moon Phases, circa 1991
Sold for $322,500 | October 2017

PART FOUR

Selling Your Collection

Romanee Conti 2005
Domaine de la Romanee Conti
3 banded owc
Bottle (9)
Sold for $152,500 | September 2017

Romanee Conti 2005
Domaine de la Romanee Conti
scl
Magnum (1)
Sold for $39,040 | September 2017

11

Selling Your Collection Through Outright Sale

This chapter is the first of three that outlines specific methods for selling your collection. There are pros and cons to each method, but the general rule for selling anything is that "time is money."

This means that, all other things being equal, the sooner that you receive payment for your collection—and the less effort you put into the sale—the less money you are likely to receive. Our goal is help you make a measured decision about the amount of time you are willing to invest in the disposition process.

Outright sale is without question the easiest method of selling a whole or partial collection. You present the articles to one or more buyers. They make offers, at which point you, as the seller, either accept or decline. The time you invest in this process is limited to the period you spend with the collectibles at the evaluation(s); if you accept an offer, you receive your payment and go on with your life. If you assembled the collection, this can be devastating or it can be cathartic, but it won't take forever.

Some people looking for a quick sale may turn to a dealer that is referred to them or advertises as specializing in sales similar to their collection. Specialized dealers may be willing to buy an entire collection. While this may be a "one-stop" quick solution, is this the best alternative for sale? If you are looking to maximize the return on value of the collection, usually the answer is no. What is the dealer thinking when you bring them your collection for a possible bid?

Dealers are in business to buy collections coming through the front door (or through the mail). Most of their advertising and their longevity at a particular site are planned specifically to create an environment that attracts such collections. Many collectibles are a fixed-supply commodity. If you're in the business, you have to acquire products to sell, and advantageous buying is at the core of such a business.

Transactions have two parties; one who wants to sell and one who wants to buy. Now comes the sticking point. In any transaction, the final result reflects the combination of knowledge and leverage of the parties. The dealer wants to buy the collection at the lowest price he or she can pay. Their leverage is that they have the money and willingness to acquire the entire collection and they also have the benefit of any degree of impatience that you possess, or that they can instill in you. You may also believe that they are more knowledgeable about current markets than you are, as a result of their experience and credentials. You, however, want to know that you are receiving the maximum reasonable price for your collectibles. Your leverage is that they do not want to let you out the door with the collection. Your knowledge and negotiating skills are also an advantage, as is any fear you can instill in the dealer about your willingness to not sell to him or her.

Another variable is location and how it affects the dealer's perception of competition. If you live in a small town with only one viable dealer and your collection does not lend itself to selling to an out-of-state or international buyer, the dealer's bid may be less competitive than you would like.

Fr. 337b $100 1878 Silver Certificate
PCGS Very Fine 35
Sold for $540,000 | January 2019

A dealer is bidding on two different kinds of items:

- First, there are those items for which they know they have customers, or which are readily liquid in their retail or "high wholesale" operations. These are items on which they can afford to accept the lowest margins, because their carrying and marketing costs will be the lowest, and their risk of not finding a buyer will be minimal.

- Second, are the articles that do not fit those criteria: collectibles that are not traded routinely and which will require greater effort to sell. This particularly applies to bulky pieces, when additional shipping weight is also a factor. Such items generally will be figured cheaply because of the effort and expense necessary to resell them at a profit. Dealers will take the time to find the "high buyer" because that is how they make a living, but their bid will reflect the effort and expense of finding a buyer and the risk of not finding a buyer.

It's easy to get upset with dealers for not reliably offering a price that is a good deal for everyone involved; ideally, you'd be able to count on the first dealer offering you what a collection is worth and that would be that. Unfortunately, it doesn't work that way—and your ability to achieve maximum value for your collection hinges on your knowledge of its value, your ability to articulate that knowledge to the dealer in a negotiation, and on your willingness to explore other options if you don't receive an offer you believe is fair.

Here are some tips for negotiating the best deal on your collection:

- **Allow Yourself a National Marketplace**
  The world has become a much smaller place through increasingly rapid communications and transportation as well as widespread Internet use. You should not limit your search for outlets to your hometown. If your collection is significant and of substantial value, potential sales outlets will come to you.

- **Find a "Full Service" Dealer**
  A large dealer with strong contacts will see your more common items as more liquid because they routinely sell this kind of material

as well as the more rare collectibles. They already know who the buyers are and what they're paying.

- **Create an "Aura of Competition"**

  It is rarely a bad idea to obtain more than one bid on something you are selling and never a bad idea to let a potential buyer know that other people are bidding. This can be communicated after you get a bid: "Is this your best offer, Mr. Smith? I know dealers sometimes leave a little 'wiggle room,' but I have two other people bidding and this isn't that kind of negotiation." It can also be communicated before the negotiation even begins: "I want you to know in advance, Mr. Smith, that I'm offering the collection for bid to three people. Please give me your best offer the first time."

- **Display Your Knowledge in Discussing the Bid**

  Dealers and people handling collectibles respect those who speak the language. You don't necessarily have to have a deep knowledge if you can "sell" a few key points. If you have a few pieces in your collection that stand out, bring them up and try to drop in a little bit of jargon from the field—perhaps some arcane reference that suggests a deeper knowledge of the field than you necessarily have.

- **"Play the Player"**

  Follow up the responses to the questions above with further questions. "You bid ____, isn't that a little low?" If the dealer can immediately address the questions with logic and explain an offer, then the offer likely is at, or at least near, its maximum. Alternatively, if he's evasive or there's no logic to his response, there's very likely negotiating room left.

- **Split the Deal**

  Rather than offer the whole collection in one lot, offer "test" groups for bid to get a feel for your potential buyers. Generally, there is more control when dealing with smaller, manageable "pieces" and more money often can be secured. There is also the "bait" technique of letting the bidders know that there is the potential for more to come. This perception may lead some bidders to treat you better in the early rounds. The trade-off is more of your time.

Historic David "Davy" Crockett's Bowie Knife Deposited to the Peale's Museum
Sold for $115,625 | June 2023

Finding the Right Venue
for the Market

When deciding where to place an item for sale, a key thing to consider is how your object will be presented by the dealer, gallery or auction house. While a six-figure painting may seem expensive, each year international auction houses sell hundreds of seven-figure paintings as part of their Impressionist, Modern and Contemporary auctions in New York and London.

Heritage's May 2, 2016, Modern and Contemporary Art sale in New York was led by Abstract Expressionist Willem de Kooning's 1968 oil on paper laid on canvas *East Hampton II*. For Heritage, the important work was able to be a star in the sale instead of just being another lot among much higher value paintings.

When selling art and collectibles, do you want your work to be featured, or do you want your work to be a lot buried in a massive catalog? For *East Hampton II*, the painting was featured prominently in a full-page advertisement in *The New York Times* and featured in a national marketing campaign. It was placed alongside a museum-quality selection of American and European works by household names including Marc Chagall, Fernand Léger, Jeff Koons, Robert Rauschenberg and Milton Avery.

The de Kooning relates to his key 1950s paintings of women. As the catalog described in vivid language, "Here, a female figure emerges from an amalgam of sweeping brushstrokes in red, orange, yellow and blue. Subtle outlines distinguish her legs and body from her surroundings. The movement of the woman's body - her lifted legs and skirt -- hints at sexual pleasure."

Your exceptional objects – no matter what collectible category they fall within – should be sold in a venue that lets it shine and advertised to a pool of bidders who can compete for it. High quality photographs, accompanying lot descriptions and essays, exhibitions to possible bidders and advertising all helps introduce a work and its qualities to potential bidders.

The result? The painting Sold for $802,000, at the top end of its estimate of $600,000 to $800,000 and more than it sold for at its last offering at auction in 2011 when offered at Sotheby's Feb. 15, 2011, auction in London.

As Heritage noted after the auction, "This sale really solidifies our position as the leaders in the middle market, giving collectors and consignors the unique opportunity to see great works, often overlooked, in an elevated evening and day sale settings."

It's tough to think of an $800,000 picture being considered in the middle market, but these types of works require a seller to ask tough questions of an auction house to help maximize value when it comes time to sell.

Willem de Kooning (1904-1997)
East Hampton II, 1968
Oil on paper laid on canvas
41-3/4 x 30 inches
Sold for $802,000 | May 2016

Frank Frazetta *Dark Kingdom*
Painting Original Art (1976).
Sold for $6,000,000 | June 2023

12

Selling Your Collectibles Through an Agent

"Sales are contingent upon the attitude of the salesman –
not the attitude of the prospect." -W. Clement Stone

The objective in choosing this method is to receive more money than you would from a direct sale. The trade-off is that it will take more time and effort—especially when enlisting the services of several agents to sell different parts of your collection.

Many people employ an agent to assist them in selling real estate. The agent knows real estate values, has methods for attracting qualified customers, and understands how to negotiate. A good dealer has the same qualifications and contacts, but you rarely hear the term "agent" being used in that context. Dealers would generally prefer to purchase collections outright, and then have the freedom to resell them without customer consultation. They may, however, accept a collection on consignment rather than lose the deal entirely.

It often is a good idea to offer a few pieces to the dealer to sell as agent to see how effectively the dealer sells, rather than handing over an entire collection all at once. This allows the agent to focus more narrowly and allows you to maintain control. The key is regular communication and interaction between you and the agent. Items that the agent has been given may not sell and must be returned. The asking price may need to be adjusted downward. Above all, you must be able to trust the agent— to have faith in the agent's ability and to be confident that your best interests are the agent's priority.

An agent is generally not worth the trouble unless they can get 10-25 percent more than you would receive in a direct sale.

The first step in seeking an agent is to determine the nature of what you plan to sell and try to match the right agent with the right product.

If your pieces are specialized, seek a specialist. If they are mainstream, look for the following kinds of qualifications:

- **Scope of Company**

  The agent (or agency) routinely handles articles of the same type, condition and values as those in your collection, and has strong customer demand for them.

- **Grading Service Experience**

  In the case of coins, the agent (or agency) regularly submits coins to the grading services and has a strong feeling for where the "standard lines" of the grades are. Ideally, the agent or other personnel in their company will have worked for a grading service and understand both the process and "looks" (eye appeal) that are most often are rewarded on marginal decisions. The same principles apply for other collectibles, such as sports cards, stamps, and certain other categories. For objects like furniture, this may not apply.

- **Regular Show Attendance**

  The agent (or agency) attends shows on a regular basis where routine contact with other collectors and dealers provides a feel for the market and provides a wide range of business contacts.

- **Web Presence and Mailing List**

  The agent has an extensive mailing (and email) list and will present your collection to the maximum number of potential buyers. It's a perfectly reasonable question to ask a dealer; top dealers are proud of the size of their contact lists.

These qualifications promise the potential of significantly higher returns, but you also want to choose an agent who genuinely seeks the role. Many dealers only want to buy and sell collectibles, and really don't have the time or inclination to assist you as an agent. Getting turned down is no reason for distress because enlisting a reluctant ally is anything but ideal. After all, an agent who acts as if selling a client's collection is some kind of favor does not have the seller's best interest at heart.

Many variables can influence the arrangement made between a seller and an agent, but these are the things that always need to be discussed:

- The agent's fees should be discussed and agreed upon in advance. Generally, an agent should receive a percentage of the selling price. This fee usually is graduated and predicated on the value of the collectibles. An agent cannot be expected to go to the trouble and expense of selling a $100 item for a commission of 5 percent. A more equitable arrangement might be a 15 percent commission on pieces valued under $1,000 and 10 percent on articles valued over that amount. This is a matter of negotiation.

- A firm minimum price for each item or group of items to be sold should be agreed upon in advance with the understanding that the seller must be advised before any articles are sold for less than this fixed price. Relinquishing a collection to an agent in exchange for a promise of an agent's best effort is not acceptable. It should be expected that the agent will do some research and make a few phone calls prior to suggesting a minimum price. Agents should be prepared to substantiate the values they suggest. Similarly, the seller should not demand unreasonable minimums. No agent worth hiring is going to waste his or her time and energy trying to sell articles that are obviously overpriced.

Duane Allman's Circa 1961/1962 Gibson SG, Cherry, Solid Body Electric Guitar, Serial #15263 Owned and Played by Graham Nash.
Sold for $591,000 | July 2019

- Agents must agree to be totally responsible for collections while it is in their possession. The agent selected may be the most honorable person on earth, but still would not be immune to theft or natural disaster. Proof of sufficient insurance coverage is mandatory. In many cases, the most prudent strategy would be to give the agent a limited number of collectibles to sell at any one time.

- Negotiating the minimums is a critical component of this kind of arrangement. If you are not comfortable with the value range of individual collectibles, it may be best to get a written offer first, which will reveal where improvement is needed before negotiating with an agent.

- Agents should be given the exclusive right to sell the collection for a specific period of time. Depending on the nature of the collection, agents may have standard practices they wish to follow. Allowing them a set length of time to sell the collection should be separated from the payment schedule. Within reason, the owner should be paid as the items are sold. A good method to use is to make periodic settlements based on time or dollar amount. If the agent is given 90 days to sell the collection, it would seem fair to request that the agent makes payments at 30 and 60-day intervals, or when the amount collected reaches $5,000 or more. We would be wary of an agent who didn't agree to this proposal. Requesting periodic payments is also a simple and positive way to measure the agent's performance.

- Finally, make sure that you have the agreement in writing. Good contracts make good trading partners, and this is a business arrangement between two parties. All terms must be spelled out and the document signed by both parties in whatever manner creates a binding contract in each state.

One other area where agents can be useful is in moving "bulk" coins. Bulk is the bane of most coin dealers' existences. Some coin collectors have accumulated 10 proof and mint sets a year for 40 years and can't understand why the dealer is not enthused when three wheelbarrows full of coin sets roll through the door. The answers are: low price and low margin plus high (relative) weight. We can virtually guarantee you that if you have an abundance of this material in your collection, it will be bid very low as part of any outright purchase offer—

probably 60-80 percent of wholesale price guides. From the dealer's perspective, it is cumbersome, difficult to process, and likely to sit gathering dust while more lucrative products are prioritized. In some cases, like with certain U.S. Mint sets, you may be receiving less than face value for the coins.

Nonetheless, there are a few dealers who specialize in the sale of this kind of material and are the "high buyers." Your agent for this kind of material should know who those high buyers are and be willing to manage the administrative functions of arranging and completing the transactions. In return, they should either receive a mutually agreed fixed fee, perhaps 5-10 percent, and expenses. You should still come out ahead of the typical direct sale offer.

In summary: match the right agent with the right material, establish realistic minimums, put the agreement in writing and communicate regularly with the agent throughout the agreement period.

> **TIPS FOR HEIRS:** If you are a non-collector and wish to use this option, we recommend that you obtain an outright purchase offer first. Use extra diligence in qualifying potential agents, and pay close attention to having the agent(s) validate the established minimum prices. Use the direct offers as a comparison and make sure that the minimums offer a significant increase. It may be even more important to offer small test groups to become more comfortable with the process and the agent.

The 48 Star Flag that Led the First Americans to Utah Beach on D-Day, June 6, 1944.
Flown from the stern of U.S. Navy vessel LCC 60 – the sole guide boat at Utah Beach–and retained by its skipper Lieutenant Howard Vander Beek.
Sold for $514,000 | June 2016

Mike Sadler's Story..........

Mike Sadler has been a consignment director with Heritage Auctions since 2003. He attended the United States Air Force Academy, flew jets for the military and is a longtime pilot with American Airlines. Before coming to Heritage Auctions, Mike's unlimited access to air travel enabled him to attend coin shows around the nation, and to build a world-class collection that was auctioned by Heritage Auctions in 2004. He is known for his tremendous knowledge of rare coins, making him a trusted colleague to many of today's most active collectors.

My journey to the greatest discovery of my career began on October 25, 2010 with a phone call from George M. Monroe, a retired Colonel in the United States Air Force. The coins he was looking to sell had been in his family for a hundred years — in a box in a closet for a substantial share of that time — and came, he was told, from an ancestor named Frank Leach.

I was intrigued enough by the call to think it was worth a trip and so the next week I landed in Washington D.C. When I walked into the meticulously kept condominium in the D.C. suburbs, I had a strong suspicion something good was about to happen, but no particular reason to think I was about to stumble into one of the greatest rare coin discoveries in U.S. history.

The provenance — directly from Frank Leach — was a big part of the appeal; President Theodore Roosevelt tapped Leach to run the United States Mint in September 1907 — a position he held until August 1909. Leach died in 1929, and 81 years later, his family was looking to sell a collection of five 1907 coins, re-designs in response to Teddy Roosevelt's disdain for American coins, which he had referred to in a 1904 letter (coincidentally, later sold by Heritage Auctions in 2012, on behalf of an entirely different consignor, for $94,000) as being possessed of "atrocious hideousness."

The rarest piece in the collection was the 1907 Rolled Edge Eagle with satin finish, in condition far superior to most of the other extant examples. I had a feeling that the 1907 Rolled Eagle was special. Not knowing anything about the transfer of rare coins, the Monroes wanted to move slowly and deliberately, making sure they realized as much value as possible for their collection. Fortunately, Col. Monroe and I bonded over my experience as a fellow United States Air Force Academy-trained military pilot, and the family trusted me enough to let me leave with the coins. When I escorted the coins back to Dallas for grading, accompanied by an armed guard, as all Heritage Auctions employees are when transporting treasures of high value, my colleagues confirmed my feeling. Heritage Auctions Senior Cataloger Mark Borckardt called it "probably the most amazing 20th century gold piece I have ever seen in my whole life." Then he added, "This coin absolutely blows my mind."

Then, (Heritage Auctions Numismatics Director), Ryan Carroll and Heritage Auctions Co-Chairman), Jim Halperin, were equally impressed; Jim said it almost had the appearance of a medal, and was unlike any of the dozens of others he'd seen. They insisted we show it to Numismatic Guaranty Corporation chairman Mark Salzberg, who happened to be in Dallas for a dealer grading event. Mark covered his eyes in disbelief when he looked at the coin. "Oh my goodness," he said. "You just don't see those like that."

One of America's smartest, most ethical coin dealers had previously offered the family $300,000 for the collection, thinking that he could make a 10-20 percent mark-up on the transaction. Heritage Auctions' argument for selling the coins at auction was simple: With specimens that were unusual and fresh to market, a public, widely advertised auction is the only method of establishing fair market value. With more common items — or pieces that have been sold recently — there is a track record on which buyers and seller can base a price. But with something like these coins from 1907, it was anyone's guess and without an auction, Col. Monroe might never know whether he had gotten full value.

Heritage experts initially had believed that the coins would fetch close to $500,000, but upon having the coins graded, realized the potential was there for very considerable upside on the Rolled Edge Eagle, which NGC finally certified as PR67.

The coins came up for sale on January 6, 2011, Platinum Night® for our annual Florida United Numismatists (FUN) auction, the largest such event of the year. Pre-sale interest had been strong, and I was able to talk the family members into making the trip to Tampa to experience the sale in person. When the hammer came down on the marquee lot — the 1907 Rolled Edge Eagle, PR67 — it brought $2,185,000, an auction record for a $10 piece, and also more than any $1, $2.50 or $5 gold coin ever had realized at auction. It was also a price far, far higher than the coin ever could have sold for in any venue other than a highly-publicized auction through a reputable major auction house with a broad base of satisfied clients. The entire consignment realized $2,564,500, and the Monroes celebrated with a glass of champagne.

As Heritage Auctions Co-Chairman Jim Halperin puts it: "Even the greatest experts often lack the imagination to predict auction values when an item is truly special."

The Estate of
Veronique and Gregory Peck

In February 2023, Heritage Auctions was honored to present Property from The Estate of Veronique and Gregory Peck, an event that paid tribute to the careers and philanthropy of the Academy Award-winning actor and his philanthropist wife of nearly 50 years. The blockbuster auction event featured numerous scripts spanning Peck's acclaimed film career, awards and notable contracts, landmark costumes, beloved works of art, and various mementos the couple accrued during their illustrious and remarkable lives.

Raoul Dufy (1877-1953). *Chevaux et turfistes à Epsom*
Watercolor, gouache, and pencil on Arches paper laid on card
19-1/2 x 25-1/2 inches (sight) © 2023 Artists Rights Society
(ARS), New York / ADAGP, Paris.
Sold for $93,750

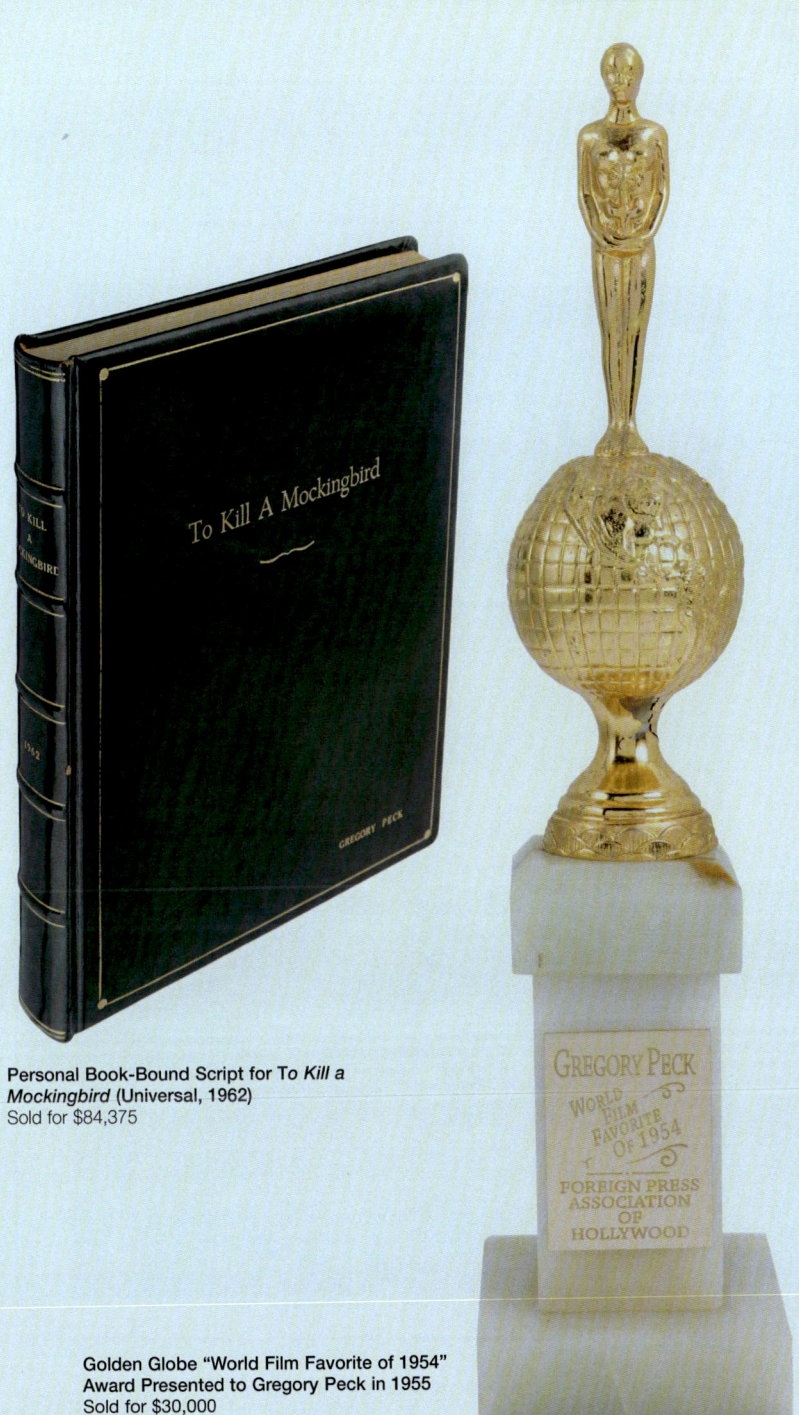

Personal Book-Bound Script for *To Kill a Mockingbird* **(Universal, 1962)**
Sold for $84,375

**Golden Globe "World Film Favorite of 1954"
Award Presented to Gregory Peck in 1955**
Sold for $30,000

Amazing Fantasy #15 (Marvel, 1962) CGC NM+ 9.6 Off-white pages.
Sold for 3,600,000 | September 2021

13

Selling Your Collection at Auction

"A fair price is the highest one a collector can
be induced to pay." – Robert Hughes

The auction always has been and forever will be the best way to show a product to as many potential customers as possible—and to ensure that you receive as much value for it as possible. When the product is rare, competing customers are important, and an auction is frequently the best venue. There are many benefits to this method of disposition, but the primary one is that in a good auction (a widely advertised one with many bidders), each item should realize at least its true worth.

An auction is a truly free market in which each article stands on its own merits. Every item is examined carefully by those most interested in it. If you have a collectible that is rare enough that it trades infrequently, its current value would have to be described as uncertain. In an outright purchase of such an item, most dealers will factor that uncertainty into their prices unless they absolutely know they have buyers at a certain level. A well-advertised sale by an established auction house, on the other hand, likely will draw the attention of all the known buyers—and any others as well. The collector community is generally a small one, and most serious buyers are aware when objects of interest are offered for sale, particularly at auction. When that condition exists, competitive demand will dictate the strongest result and produce the truest value for a particular collectible.

Finally, esoteric items—those that are not traded routinely—may again bring the very best price at an auction. At the very least, a well-publicized auction through a reputable auction house will instill the peace of mind that your item was exposed to every buyer possible in a transparent way, even if it didn't lead to a price as high as you had hoped. Choose an auctioneer with a strong track record for the particular genre—one who has the clientele (both mailing list and attendance) and auction locations to put the collection in front of the greatest number of potential buyers. When looking for an auctioneer, consider the following qualifications:

- ## Financial Resources and Stability
  An auction consignment is first and foremost a business deal. As with contracting an agent, auctioneers must demonstrate sufficient financial resources to ensure they can both effectively conduct the sale and pay sellers at the stated settlement date. They also must accept liability and provide full insurance against the loss or damage of a collection.

- ## Longevity in the Business
  An auction house is a complex operation that requires a great deal of development to assure everything flows smoothly: consignor and bidder bases, cataloging references and expertise, site setup and physical security, auction flow and administrative efficiency-flows—and that only begins to touch on what goes into it. Go with a proven entity; after all, it's your money that's involved.

- ## Advertising Resources
  Success breeds success. You can't have the top sales without great advertising, and vice versa. Look for the companies who are doing the major advertising in the trade papers and on the Internet.

- ## Location
  The auction business is no different than many other businesses, an important faction is location, location, location. That said, the last several decades, with increase use and reliance on the internet, while geographic location has taken less importance, location is still a factor. The key is finding a company with national and international reach either through physical presence or the internet. A company that is limited to holding auctions in locations out of the mainstream does not have the ability to attract a large bidder base. The key for live auctions is the ability hold auctions in major financial centers with good regional access. When considering a company that holds online auctions, or deals exclusively online, comparing web traffic rankings of different auctioneers can provide an indicator of web presence and the ability to reach a broad market.

Spacecraft ID plate from Apollo 11's Lunar Module *Eagle*
Apollo 11 Lunar Module Flown Spacecraft Identification
Sold for $468,500 | November 2018
Plate Display Directly From The Armstrong Family Collection™

- ## Competitive Rates

   Auction companies charge both buyer's and seller's fees to absorb the expenses of the sale and turn a profit. A seller's fee of 15 to 20% has become the standard and you should not have to pay more, unless your collection has extraordinary "bulk" or requires special attention. Indeed, if you have a significant collection, you may be able to negotiate a better rate.

- ## Strong Writing and Imaging
  Catalog descriptions and photography create the necessary excitement and demand for an auction's collectibles and provide all that is available to entice bidders who cannot attend the sale in person. Our company, Heritage Auctions, is a pioneer in the use of online videos and extensive descriptions presented through the Internet as alternative cataloging media. It's clear that this is the wave of the future. Browse through the listings on an auctioneer's website and look at the photos and catalog descriptions for lots that are in the same price range as what you're looking to sell. If you were the seller of those pieces, would you be happy with the merchandising efforts?

- ## Professional Personnel
  It takes quality personnel—and many of them—to conduct a great auction. In qualifying auctioneers, be certain to inquire as to the number of people that will be involved in managing your consignment and what their roles are. Our company provides potential consignors with a video that details the auction process from start to finish, and other companies should at least have literature that covers the same ground. Any company is only as good as its people. Contact a number of reputable auction houses to get an impression as to how they will treat your collection. Also, read through the listings of employees on different auctioneers' websites. Do they have specialists with impressive resumes in the category you're looking to sell in?

Auction is often the best venue for high-quality collectibles, particularly if the items trade infrequently. A good auction attracts the right mix of bidders to establish the real value for each individual piece.

If this seems the best route for you, interview potential auctioneers to determine which of them combines the best business resources, venues and personnel assets. Some things to consider:

- Ask the auctioneer's Consignment Director to evaluate your collection and make recommendations on which articles should be auctioned and which would be better sold by another method. Ask them to explain why.

- Do you wish to be recognized for your collecting achievements? Some consignors prefer anonymity, but if you desire recognition, becoming a signature consignor involves two factors:

  - Your overall collection must be of significant value. This could vary from auction to auction, but for a rough figure, let's use $250,000.

  - Alternatively, you may have an interesting collection of a more specific focus—possibly all items are in one group or category. Don't hesitate to ask, particularly if there's a good story behind the collection!

- From an auctioneer's perspective, a few high-value items are preferable to a large collection of lower-value pieces, even if the total value is the same: the workload is lower. You might be able to negotiate a lower seller's fee if you have the "right" kind of material.

- Large lots are at the other end of the spectrum. Large lots are bulky, cumbersome to carry to auction sites and difficult to ship once sold. They are time-consuming to catalog and require a lot of extra effort to earn the same percentage as a single piece of comparable lot value. Auction company personnel are not very fond of the large lots in major auctions and neither are most bidders, because their focus is on the more "high-powered" lots. Auctioneers will take your large lots for a big sale, but you have absolutely no leverage, and that's not what auctions are all about. In most cases, you would be better off asking the auctioneer to bid the large lots straight up. You will probably realize greater net proceeds and will be paid immediately.

- Keep in mind that the lowest commission rate is not necessarily the best deal. The first consideration should be the auctioneer's ability to provide your collection with maximum exposure and promotion. Saving an extra percentage point or two is meaningless if another auctioneer could secure an extra 20 percent for your collection. Negotiate the best possible commission you can once you've found the best auction house for your collectibles; don't pick an auction house based solely on the commission.

**Republic Chang Tso-lin silver Pattern "Mukden Tiger" Dollar Year 17 (1928)
MS62 NGC**
Sold for $2,160,000 | December 202

- Auction house will usually provide estimates of where they believe items will sell based on their client bases and experience. Some seller chose to list their collectibles unrestricted and others place a "reserve" price to ensure an item is not sold for less than a final price they would be comfortable receiving. While reserves provide a "floor", there are drawbacks to consider. Not having a reserve could attract more bidders, which is a benefit of auctions. As people are bidding, they can get caught up in the moment, a the competition of not being outbid can drive hammer prices (the final bid amount) up. In addition, if an item is not sold with a reserve, the seller could face the prospect of paying buy=back fees and reserve fees. These are generally fees charged by auction houses to cover their marketing and other out of pocket costs that they usually would recoup from buyer's premiums on items sold at auction. If you've carefully selected an auction house that will provide your pieces with maximum exposure, a reserve should not be necessary If a reserve is used, generally, the reserve fee is a percentage is based on the overall terms of your consignment and how realistic the auctioneer thinks your reserves are. You should expect the reserve fee to be 5-10 percent. If the amount is more than that, ask for an explanation. Good auction houses are likely to be knowledgeable about what an item can reasonably be expected to bring and if they tell you your proposed reserve is too high, pay attention.

- Ask the consignment coordinator for the cost of photography and lotting in the auctions that you are considering. For example, in some auctions, the minimum value for a catalog photograph may be $1,500 and in others, $2,500. The latter auction, while possibly a better venue overall, might not be as beneficial for your pieces valued from $1,500 to $2,400. Similarly, each auction will have a minimum lot value. In some cases, it's $250, sometimes it's $500, and in the very best of sales, it may be $1,000. Most auction companies will allow you to combine items to reach the minimum, but there is a limit to the number that may be used and still receive individual, mainstream placement. The key point for you to remember is that if your overall consignment is a good one, you may be able to negotiate a more lenient lot and photography standard.

Marketing at Work   The Harry Potter Chair

When a unique item with broad popular appeal comes to auction, anything can happen. Such was the case with the chair that J.K. Rowling sat upon while writing the first two books in the *Harry Potter* series. It was painted and signed by Rowling herself.

As CNN observed, "At first glance, it looks like a shabby, wooden chair with colorful graffiti scrawled on it." But those scribbles say, "You may not / find me pretty / but don't judge / on what you see," and "I wrote / Harry Potter / while sitting / on this chair." "Gryffindor" is painted on the cross stretcher under the seat.

The catalog description described the chair's history in vivid detail: "During her days as an impoverished single mother in Edinburgh, J.K. Rowling was given a free set of four chairs for her council flat – a social housing unit provided by the British government. This set included a standard 1930's-era oak chair with a replacement burlap seat decorated with a red thistle. The latter being one of the more comfortable chairs amongst the bunch, she favored it to sit in whilst writing the first drafts of *Harry Potter and the Philosopher's Stone* and *Harry Potter and the Chamber of Secrets* – the first two books of a seven part series that would become an international phenomenon."

The chair would be donated to a small auction in 2002 called Chair-ish a Child in aid of the National Society for the Prevention of Cruelty to Children (NSPCC) where it sold for $21,000. For this auction, Rowling used gold, rose, and green paints to transform the chair into a magical piece of literary memorabilia, fearing that the chair in its original form would look like it had been "purchased from a junk shop for a tenner."

When it traded next in 2009 in an eBay auction benefiting the charitable organization Books Abroad, it sold for the U.S. equivalent of nearly $30,000. It was purchased by Gerald Gray, the CEO of AutoKontrol USA, who consigned it with Heritage in 2016. Gray planned to donate 10 percent of the winning price to Lumos, Rowling's children's charity.

Heritage shared the story with media outlets around the world, a physical object representative of a woman's against-all-odds struggle to share her creative vision. In a letter accompanying the chair, Rowling said, "My nostalgic side is quite sad to see it go, but my back isn't."

As part of Heritage Auction's global public relations campaign, the chair went on display at its Park Avenue, New York, office on a custom rotating platform. For weeks, families posed for photos with what is arguably the most important piece of *Harry Potter* memorabilia that exists. The $394,000 it brought at Heritage on April 6, 2016, was many multiples of its opening bid of $45,000. The winning bidder, who elected to remain anonymous, also received Rowling's signed letter "by Owl Post" describing the history and provenance.

Gray, who attended the auction at the Waldorf Astoria hotel in New York City hoped that it would eventually go on display where fans could appreciate it. But even if it stays in a private collection, through extensive marketing, Heritage was able to share the story of this magical chair with millions of Harry Potter fans.

Chair Used by J.K. Rowling whilst Writing the First Two *Harry Potter* Books, Later Hand-Painted and Signed by Rowling Herself.
Sold for $394,000 | April 2016

Internet Auctions

Online auction websites like eBay allow you to sell your items at auction yourself, with exposure to a wide variety of bidders at a commission far lower than what you would pay trough a traditional auction house. The question is whether this is a good idea. Consider the following questions:

- Do you already have a "feedback" rating that will give you credibility with the bidder base? Many Internet auction bidders are concerned about online deal-making with people they don't know. The equalizer is the feedback system that lets buyers and sellers build online reputations. If you don't have a feedback rating, many bidders will avoid your auctions altogether and others will bid less.

- Do you have the equipment and skill to create digital images of the articles to be auctioned? Items without high-quality images just don't sell as well. For quality coin photography, you'll need a digital camera and the knowledge to upload those photos.

- Do you have the skills to write descriptions for each item? Do you know enough about the piece—and how to grade condition—to describe it? Auction bidders are best motivated when a "story" is available to make the collectible more interesting. The visual image and description provide the combination that maximizes an Internet auction's results.

- Do you have the business skills to analyze potential problem situations? Can you collect a bad check or determine whether a "special request" from a customer is legitimate or a scam? Most of the people on the Internet are honest, but there are exceptions. Unfortunately, it doesn't take many bad deals to turn a profitable situation into a loss.

- Do you have the knowledge and resources to ship high-dollar packages to 100 different people? It takes a thorough knowledge of postal regulations and requirements, a considerable amount of shipping materials and insurance, and a great deal of organization and time.

- Do you really want to sell collectibles that might have upside potential in an Internet-only venue? More to the point, are you able to ascertain which pieces might have that upside potential?

We routinely advise would-be consignors to list certain items on eBay: Hummel figurines, common post-1970 baseball cards, and small quantities of items that aren't rare enough to justify a consignment to a full-service auction house. But for high-value items that require specialized marketing or a seller with credibility in the field, we aren't shy about saying it: auctions are the way to go.

TIPS FOR HEIRS AND ADVISORS: A reputable auction house can be the best option for Trusts, Estates and heirs faced with need for liquidity (for taxes, equitable division of assets, etc.) or simply the desire to sell off a collection. This is especially true for individuals with little or no knowledge of collectibles and are concerned about receiving fair value. When selling at auction, the best interests of the seller are intrinsically intwined with the the auctioneer as the auctioneer will receive a buyer's premium, which is a percentage of the final sale price. : the more money you make, the more money they make. Additionally, the values will be established by third parties in the competitive bidding process. The real benefit of engaging a major auction house is its versatility. Summing up all of the methods of disposition, certain collectibles are better suited for one method, while others would benefit more from a different venue. A major company should be willing to recommend the best venue for each of your pieces and divide the collection to your best advantage. Just be sure to ask. Heritage's Trusts & Estates Department assists in just such situations and can coordinate the sale of an estate through various venues and categories of property to realize the best return on the sale of a collection. Please visit HA.com/Estates.

Oscar Heyman Diamond, Ruby, Emerald, Gold Brooch
Sold for $40,000 | December 2021
Property from the Estate of Kittie West Nelson Ferguson

14

.
.
.
.
.
.

Etiquette & Tips

"Tact is one of the first mental virtues, the absence
of it is fatal to the best talent." – William Gilmore Simms

"Etiquette means behaving yourself a little better
than is absolutely essential." – Will Cuppy

The purpose of this book is to help you plan for the future and, if you wish, to help you maintain and dispose of your collection without being taken advantage of by the dealers and other collectors and give you a basic understand of government rules and regulations so you know your rights and will be able to engage with your advisors in a meaningful way.

It is reasonable to assume that you want to receive as much money for your collection as possible. Similarly, it is reasonable to believe that potential buyers would want to pay the least amount they can. The one thing that is absolutely certain is that everyone else will maximize his or her own interests. You should, too.

There are certain rules of etiquette within any collectibles community. The first premise is the division of roles. If you present yourself as a dealer, you are automatically responsible for all your actions and decisions in the arena of that collectible. That means if you make a mistake, you live with it. It also imparts a certain level of responsibility toward those who are not dealers. Dealers trade with each other at wholesale levels, in part because they communicate in the same form of verbal shorthand that assumes a level of expertise. A collectible is presented, offered, inspected and purchased (or not) without fanfare, and the principals move on to the next deal.

Conversely, many collectors ask a lot of questions (and rightly so), are nervous about their acquisitions, and return a portion of those purchases after the sale. In return for this extra "maintenance," dealers charge collectors more and pay them less than they would another dealer. It is the way of the business, and perfectly justifiable, as there have to be both retail and wholesale levels for any market to function. Naturally, most collectors would like to purchase at wholesale, and occasionally, they are awarded that opportunity. Usually, the key to this is demonstrating a familiarity with wholesale market levels, negotiating pleasantly and well, and asking only pertinent questions.

The same is true on the selling side. If you give others the impression that you know what you are doing, you will receive the best bid or options the first time around. We recommend, however, that you do not present yourself as a dealer. Some collectors claim to be "vest pocket" dealers in hopes of receiving higher offers. Usually, this backfires, as the dealer then feels relieved of any obligation he may have to point out to you unrecognized rarities. Be upfront, but be competent.

As a non-professional, you should be able to expect:

• An appointment to allow sufficient time to evaluate your collection.

• Financial and industry references at your request (and you should request them).

• Professional treatment of you and your collection, and quality security.

• You should request (prior) that any items bid at $1,000 or more be identified singly and that any article that would benefit from certification be listed.

• A written offer presented in a timely manner. The offer should be dated and any deadline noted.

• If the company has an auction house as well, and you request it, recommendations on which collectibles are better suited for auction or direct sale should also be listed.

• Prompt payment in good funds if the offer is accepted. If the collection is sold at auction, payment in good funds on the settlement date as promised.

The dealer has a right to expect certain conduct from you as well:

• That you keep any scheduled appointment and are prompt. This applies to the dealer and their staff as well.

- The collection should be as organized as possible to minimize the time necessary to evaluate and bid on it. Even a basic inventory indicating the location of each item is helpful. If the collection lends itself to grouping, this should be done beforehand. If one group out of the collection contains most of the "value," it can be presented separately.

- You should not "shop" the dealer's offer to other dealers. It's okay to tell each bidder that other bids are being sought, but you should neither reveal what the other bids are, nor the details of who is bidding. Shopping an offer for a few more dollars is strictly "bush league," and it can definitely backfire. For example, if your first bidder did not make a strong bid and you reveal the number, the second bidder may play the competition instead of the real value and you will come up short. Similarly, if you reveal the identity of those you plan to see, the bidders could collude with one another to your disadvantage. Remember, the aura of unknown competition is the strongest leverage you have to inspire dealers to figure the deal closely and make their best bids.

- You should tell the dealer "yes" or "no" in a reasonable amount of time, and that applies even if you accept another bid. It would be considerate for you to let them know the winning bid. They can learn from the experience and not feel that their time was wasted. That can be to your advantage as well, because if you bring back more collectibles for them to bid, they should both appreciate your professionalism and bid higher the next time.

Above all, you should both expect and extend courtesy. Do not waste time with a dealer who is discourteous, nor waste time responding. Ask and answer questions, but beware of becoming agitated, even if you disagree with something you hear. Your mission is to obtain the greatest possible price for your collection. To accomplish this, it is usually best to reserve judgment until all of the information has been gathered. The very person you disagreed with may be the highest overall bidder.

One final option for selling: Occasionally people ask us why they shouldn't dispose of their collectibles to, or through, another collector. The premise is that the collector would pay more and the playing field would be more level. There is some general merit to those statements, but there are some caveats as well:

- A collector will pay more for some items, but will rarely pay more for all of them. Take care that you don't receive a little more for the best few pieces of your collection only to find that there are no buyers for the less favorable material.

- Being a collector in and of itself is no guarantee that the individual you contact is any more or less knowledgeable or ethical than a dealer. In general, dealers are better-informed on current market conditions, upgrade potential and the reputations of potential buyers. We know of at least one situation where a collector acquaintance sold a collection for heirs, only to take a bad check from the buyer. That individual was well known as a "bad egg" by the dealer community, but the collector/agent was totally unaware. It took more than a year and considerable expense for the heirs to collect a fraction of the amount owed.

- As an agent, the collector is less likely to have insurance coverage for your collection while in their care. If you use a collector, don't forget to verify this just as you would with a dealer.

- Most importantly, few collectors will truly be interested in acquiring everything you have—and if they are willing to buy in bulk from you, it will likely only be because they are interested in getting a great deal.

The bottom line is that you should qualify a collector in the same manner as you would a dealer. Although collectors may have good intentions, a major collection should be sold only with the assistance of a qualified professional. It is unwise to rely on a part-time hobbyist to dispose of a major financial asset; a better approach is to use an auction to let that collector bid against tens of thousands of similar hobbyists.

Preserving Your Legacy - Heir Best Practice

The final note to leave you with would be the best practices for preserving your legacy collection is good communication during life or after death with your heirs and those that will control your estate/trust when you are not able to do so yourself. Collectors, as the owners, have all the rights and responsibilities for the collection in their lifetimes, and can provide as much or as little guidance as they please. If the collector desires for their heirs to retain and appreciate their collections, they should engage with their heir during their life and explain to them what they have acquired and why. In addition, careful thought should be given to who should get what when the collector passes. Any

**A Pair of French Napoleon III Gilt Bronze Mounted Covered Urns
on Fluted Rouge Marble Columns, 19th century**
Sold for $106,250 | August 2021
Property from the Estate of Phyllis McGuire, Las Vegas, Nevada

guidance is better than no guidance. Failing to provide guidance can lead to unnecessary family disharmony, forced sale of collections and the loss of the legacy the collector was looking to pass one.

Best practice would be for the collectors to identify and detail any specific bequests they wish to make. "Dad split them up that way in the will or trust" is a lot more powerful than "I'm sure Dad wanted me to have this one."

Similarly, the collector should indicate who should be contacted to help dispose of the collection—and who should not. It's amazing how many "old friends" can appear after the death of a known collector. The executor or trustee, whether he or she is a family member or not, should be advised of all these details.

Heirs should remember that the other heirs are also probably under a great deal of stress—so try to give everyone the benefit of the doubt. We like to think that family is the most important thing, so here are some tips to avoid controversy if the collection needs to be sold or disposed of equitably when specific guidance was not provided by the deceased:

• Leave the division to a third party. If the collection is not to be sold, have the appraiser separate the inventory into the appropriate number of groups by value.

• If one or more heirs want specific pieces, have the appraiser value those individually and if the remainder of the collection is sold, use those amounts to adjust shares accordingly.

• If the collection is to be disposed of, but each heir wants "something" to remember the deceased by, determine the dollar value that you want to set aside and have each heir "buy" the collectibles they want at the appraised price.

• In all cases, remember to keep things in perspective. The collection once provided a great deal of pleasure to your loved one, and try to let its legacy reflect that.

The preparation of this handbook has been a labor of love, though by no means easy. There are two main reader groups that have been targeted by this treatise, neither of whom should be overjoyed by the implications of having to read through it. If you are a collector, the thought of estate planning may make you look closer at your own mortality. If you are an heir or possible heir of a collector, contemplating a loved one's mortality is probably no more enjoyable.

We would take more pleasure in relating a more upbeat subject, but we will be satisfied if this handbook has made it a little easier for you to address a very difficult task.

We offer, in closing, this final guidance regardless of your circumstance or role:

1. Determine your goal.
2. Know your options.
3. Analyze them and pick the best course of action for you.
4. Make a plan.
5. If you need assistance, choose it carefully.
6. Above all, remain flexible and don't be afraid to adjust your plan as you go along.
7. Form a team of the best advisors available and pay the price now rather than later.

Good luck!

G. (Gerald Harvey Jones) Harvey (American, 1933-2017)
When Cowboys Don't Change, 1993
Oil on canvas
40 x 60 inches
Sold for $516,500 | November 2018
WORLD AUCTION RECORD FOR THE ARTIST

Jim Halperin's Story . . . .

Jim Halperin is the co-founder and co-chairman of Heritage Auctions. He formed his first rare coin business at the age of 16, then dropped out of Harvard in December 1971 to pursue a career in numismatics. He also is the author of two bestselling futurist novels, and endows The James & Gayle Halperin Foundation, which supports health and education-related charities. You can view his personal collections at: www.jhalpe.com.

Even though I callously had disappointed my dad by deciding not to graduate from his alma mater, he remained steadfastly supportive. By 1975, at age 22, I was ready to computerize my growing coin business in Framingham, Massachusetts, and my dad, who at the time was 49 years old and had sold his own successful manufacturing business a decade earlier, offered to come in part-time and help me. I jumped at the offer. Together we set up the first full-fledged computer system in the coin business, an IBM 360 mainframe, and when we were finished, he had an idea — a sort of parting gift soon before he and my mom would begin spending most of their time in Florida.

My dad's idea was to set up a rare coin fund; he would recruit investors to buy shares in a limited partnership, and I would use the money to buy coins, store them in a safe deposit box, wait a few years, and then sell them at auction. Using his many contacts — and cold-calling on, among others, Fidelity Investments founder Ned Johnson, who invested $30,000 on the spot — he quickly raised $375,000. We called it the New England Rare Coin Fund. Now all I had to do was buy the coins. Having worked in the business since I was 16, I spent about 18 months slowly acquiring high-grade American rarities because I knew that those were the coins that sold the fastest whenever we had them available. I bought only specimens that I would have loved to own but couldn't have otherwise afforded to keep in inventory.

The economy had been in a moderate recovery when I'd bought the coins, but when it was time to sell a few years later, the timing could not have been better. By 1980, the Iran hostage crisis was under way, inflation had soared to 13.5 percent, and bank failures were heading toward the highest levels seen since the Great Depression. Unemployment was over 7 percent. Investors — from hedge funds to retirees — were seeking scarce physical objects unencumbered by complex financing arrangements, with aesthetic and historical significance that no oil crisis could ever taint.

When the collection was sold at auction in April of 1980, our investors in attendance stared in disbelief. Those same coins generated more than $2.15 million and, after all commissions, expenses and fees, every investor who put in $15,000 got back more than $69,000. This, at a time when they had been watching most or all of their other investments tank. The profits from our little coin fund rescued businesses, saved homes, and even helped a couple of our investors avoid filing bankruptcy.

I was now 27 years old, and the experience would help me develop my own philosophy about investments — and the importance of owning a portfolio that Nassim Nicholas Taleb, the internationally bestselling author/hedge fund manager/philosopher, has recently termed "antifragile." That is, a basket that encompasses a diversity of assets, including some that are debt-free and likely to gain in value just as the world around them is collapsing.

Of course, there are many ways to diversify assets — but including some treasures that provide their owners with joy and beauty is, for my money, one of the best.

Joseph Christian Leyendecker (American, 1874-1951)
Beat-up Boy, Football Hero, The Saturday Evening Post cover, November 21, 1914
Sold for $4,121,250 | May 2021

APPENDICES

APPENDIX A

ORGANIZATIONS FOR COLLECTORS

Autographs

Universal Autograph Collectors Club
UACC P.O. Box 1392
Mount Dora, FL 32756
uacc.org

Founded in 1965, this non-profit organization publishes a quarterly journal and offers information on authentication and recommended dealers, and a list of dealers it recommends consumers avoid.

Coins

American Numismatic Association (ANA)
818 North Cascade Avenue
Colorado Springs, CO 80903
719-632-2646
E-mail: ana@money.org
money.org

The American Numismatic Association is the country's largest collector organization for coins and related items. Formed in 1891, the ANA offers extensive educational programs and a monthly magazine, *The Numismatist*. Its Colorado Springs headquarters features a first-rate museum and library that are available to members and non- members alike. The ANA offers renowned summer seminars on a number of numismatic subjects and holds two conventions annually. These shows offer 250 to 500 bourse tables and significant auctions. The annual convention auction (held in July or August) is frequently the highest-grossing auction sale of the year.

Professional Numismatists Guild (PNG)
28441 Rancho California Rd., Suite 106
Temecula, CA 92590
951-587-8300
E-mail: info@pngdealers.com
pngdealers.com

The Professional Numismatists Guild is the preeminent dealer group in the coin industry. Formed in 1955 with the motto, "Knowledge, Integrity, Responsibility," the PNG accepts members only after stringent background and financial investigations, and a vote of the entire membership. Members agree to uphold a strict code of ethics and to resolve any complaints against them through binding PNG arbitration. A list of PNG dealers is available from the organization.

American Numismatic Society (ANS)

75 Varick Street, 11th floor
New York, NY 10013
212 571 4470
E-mail: info@amnumsoc.org
amnumsoc.org

The American Numismatic Society was founded in 1858, and is dedicated to the serious study of numismatic items. To that end, it has an extensive research library and world-class collections, and provides members and visiting scholars with a broad selection of publications, topical meetings and symposia, fellowships and grants, honors and awards, and various educational projects.

Minerals

The Mineralogical Society of America

3635 Concorde Pkwy Suite 500
Chantilly, VA 20151-1110
703-652-9950
Email: business@minsocam.org;
minsocam.org

It's not Heritage's biggest or best-known category—but it's pretty cool: minerals and meteorites. Individual pieces in our past minerals sales have sold for more than half a million dollars. The Mineralogical Society of America, foundedin 1919, offers magazines, books, and educational programs for the general public.

Topaz
Xanda Mine, Virgem da Lapa
Minas Gerais, Brazil
Sold for $200,000 | August 2019

Stamps

American Philatelic Society (APS)

100 Match Factory Place
Bellefonte, PA 16823
814-933-3803
E-mail: webmaster@stamps.org;
stamps.org

The American Philatelic Society was founded in 1886 and offers members a monthly magazine, an authentication service, educational opportunities, and much more. Through a partnership with Hugh Wood, Inc. and The Chubb Group of Insurance Companies, it also offers a service for insuring stamp collections.

APPENDIX B

INSURANCE COMPANIES OFFERING SPECIALIZED COVERAGE FOR COLLECTORS

COLLECTIBLE AND NUMISMATIC COVERAGE

Cleland & Associates
3419 Westminster Ave. #301G
Dallas, TX 75205
409-766-7101
Contact: Richard Cleland
coininsurance.com

North American Collectibles Association
3002 Hempland Rd. Suite B
Lancaster, PA 17601-1362
800-685-6746
Contact: Barbara Wingo
nacacollectors.com

Hugh Wood, Inc.
(American Agent for
Lloyds of London)
One Exchange Plaza
55 Broadway, 24th Floor
New York, NY 10006
212-509-3777
Contact: Jack Fisher
hughwood.com

SEARCH EACH OF THESE NATIONAL WEBSITES FOR AN AGENT OR BROKER NEAREST YOU

American International Group
(formerly Chartis)
Private Client Group
aigpcg.com

AXA Art Insurance
212-415-8400
axa-art.com

**Chubb Group
of Insurance Companies**
866-324-8222
chubb.com

**Huntington T. Block
Insurance Agency**
800-424-8830
huntingtontblock.com

Pure Insurance
888-813-7873
pureinsurance.com

Marsh Private Client Services
pcs.marsh.com

Dale Chihuly (American, b. 1941)
Cobalt Macchia with Huckleberry Lip Wrap, 2003
Blown Glass
16-1/2 x 35 x 31 inches
Sold for $37,500 September 2021
Property from the Estate of Richard L. Weisman, Beverly Hills, California

HUMPHREY
OGART

INGRID
RGMAN

PAUL
NREID

avevano l'annuntamento· col destino a

CASABLANCA

Casablanca (Warner Brothers, 1946).
**First Post-War Release Italian 4 – Fogli
(55.5" X 78.25") Luigi Martinati Artwork.
Sold for $478,000 | July 2017**

CLAUDE
RAINS ·

CONRAD
VEIDT

SYDNEY
GREENSTREET ·

PETER
LORRE

Regis :
MICHAEL CURTIZ

Warner Bros.

APPENDIX C
THIRD-PARTY GRADING SERVICES

BASEBALL CARDS

Sportscard Guaranty Corporation (SGC)
951 Yamato Rd, Suite 110
Boca Raton, FL 33431
800-SGC-9212
973-984-0018
sgccard.com/grading-fees

Professional Sports Authenticator (PSA)
P.O. Box 6180
Newport Beach, CA 92658
800-325-1121,
949-833-8824
Email: info@psacard.com
Beckett Grading Services (BGS)
beckett.com/grading

COINS

Numismatic Guaranty Corporation of America (NGC)
P.O. Box 4776
Sarasota, FL 34230
800-NGC-COIN
941-360-3990
ngccoin.com

ANACS
P.P.O. Box 6000
Englewood, CO 80155
800-888-1861
anacs.com

Professional Coin Grading Service (PCGS)
P.O. Box 9458
Newport Beach, CA 92658
800-447-8848
949-833-0600
pcgs.com

COINS NEEDING CLEANING OR CONSERVATION

Numismatic Conservation Services (NCS)
P.O. Box 4750
Sarasota, FL 34230
1-866-627-2646
1-941-360-3996
ncscoin.com

COMICS

Comics Guaranty Corporation (CGC)
P.O. Box 4738
Sarasota, FL 34230
1-877-NM-COMIC
1-941-360-3991
FAX: 941-360-2558
cgccomics.com

CURRENCY

Paper Money Grading (PMG)
P.O. Box 4755
Sarasota, FL 34230
877-PMG-5570
941 309 1001
PMGnotes.com

PCGS Banknote
P.O. Box 9458
Newport Beach, CA 92658
800-447-8848
www.pcgs.com/banknote

APPENDIX D

SELECTED PUBLICATIONS FOR COLLECTORS

Artwork & Paper Collectibles

How to Care for Works of Art on Paper,
by Francis W. Dolloff and Roy L. Perkinson

Conservation Concerns: A Guide for Collectors and Curators, by Konstanze Bachmann, Dianne Pilgrim

Caring for Your Art, by Jill Snyder, Joseph Montague, Maria Reidelbach

Baseball Cards

The Official Price Guide to Baseball Cards, by James Beckett

Books & Manuscripts

Antiquarian Booksellers Association of American (ABAA.org) posts links to member-published books and articles on collecting Rare Books and Manuscripts

How to Identify and Collect American First Editions, Arco Publishing, New York (1976) – (out of print; you'll probably have to find a rare copy)

We also recommend: ABEBooks.com as a source of books on the Internet

Coins

The New York Times Guide to Coin Collecting: Do's, Don'ts, Facts, Myths, and a Wealth of History, by Ed Reiter

How to Grade U.S. Coins, by James L. Halperin

A Guide Book of United States Coins, by R. S. Yeoman

The Standard Catalog of World Coins, by Chester Krause & Clifford Mishler

Comics

The Official Overstreet Comic Book Price Guide, by Robert M. Overstreet (available digitally at HeritageComics.com)

Furniture

The Bulfinch Anatomy of Antique Furniture: An Illustrated Guide to Identifying Period, Detail, and Design, by Tim Forrest, Paul Atterbury

American Antique Furniture: A Book for Amateurs,
Vol. 1., by Jr. Edgar G. Miller

Miller's Collecting Furniture: Facts at Your Fingertips, by Christopher Payne

Guns

The Gun Digest Book of Modern Gun Values: For Modern Arms Made from 1900 to Present (16th Ed.), by Phillip Peterson

Standard Catalog of Military Firearms: The Collector's Price and Reference Guide (6h Ed.), by Phillip Peterson

Antique Guns: The Collector's Guide, by John E. Traister

Jewelry

Signed Beauties of Costume Jewelry: Identification & Values, by Marcia Sparkles Brown

Vintage Jewelry: A Price and Identification Guide, 1920 to 1940s, by Leigh Leshner

Antique Trader Jewelry Price Guide, by Kyle Husfloen and Marion Cohen

Paintings & Sculpture

AskART.com

ArtNet.com

Toys

Official Hake's Price Guide to Character Toys, by Ted Hake

Cartoon Toys & Collectibles Identification and Value Guide, by David Longest

All Collectibles & Fine Arts

Maloney's Antiques & Collectibles Resource Directory, by David J. Maloney, Jr.

Warman's Antiques & Collectibles 2016 Price Guide, by Noah Fleischer

For additional resources in all collector categories, please visit our Resources list at HA.com, where we also invite you to take our Collector Survey to qualify for free auction catalogs and a drawing to win valuable prizes.

La Tache 1988
Domaine de la Romanee Conti
The Estate of a Pennsylvania Gentleman
Sold for $44,280 | September 2022

About the Authors

James L. Halperin

Born in Boston in 1952, Jim formed a part-time rare stamp and coin business at age 16. The same year, he received early acceptance to Harvard College. But by his third semester, Jim was enjoying the coin business more than his studies, so he took a permanent leave of absence to pursue a full-time numismatic career. In 1975, Jim supervised the protocols for the first mainframe computer system in the numismatic business, which would help catapult his firm to the top of the industry within four years. In 1982, Jim's business merged with that of his friend and former archrival Steve Ivy to form Heritage. In 1984, Jim wrote a book later re-titled "How to Grade U.S. Coins", which outlined the grading standards upon which NGC and PCGS would later be based. Jim is also a well-known futurist, an active collector of rare comic books, comic art and early 20th-century American art (view parts of his collection www.jhalpe.com), venture capital investor, philanthropist (he endows a multimillion-dollar health education foundation), and part-time novelist. His first fiction book, "The Truth Machine", was published in 1996, became an international science fiction bestseller, was optioned as a feature film by Warner Brothers, and is now under development at Lions Gate. Jim's second novel, "The First Immortal", was published in early 1998 and optioned as a Hallmark Hall of Fame television miniseries. All of Jim's royalties are donated to health and education charities.

Gregory J. Rohan

At the age of eight, Greg Rohan started collecting coins and by 1971, at the age of 10, he was buying and selling coins from a dealer's table at trade shows in his hometown of Seattle. His business grew rapidly, and in 1987, he joined Heritage as Executive Vice-President. Today, as a partner and as President of Heritage, his responsibilities include overseeing the firm's private client group and working with top collectors in every field in which Heritage is active. Greg has been involved with many of the rarest items and most important collections handled by the firm, including the purchase and/or sale of the Ed Trompeter Collection (the world's largest numismatic purchase according to the Guinness Book of World Records). During his career, Greg has handled more than $1 billion of rare coins, collectibles and art. He has provided expert testimony for the United States Attorneys in San Francisco, Dallas, and Philadelphia, and for the Federal Trade Commission (FTC). He has worked with collectors, consignors, and their advisors regarding significant collections of books, manuscripts, comics, currency, jewelry, vintage movie posters, sports and entertainment memorabilia, decorative arts, and fine art, to name just a few. Greg is a past Chapter Chairman for North Texas of the Young Presidents' Organization (YPO), and is an active supporter of the arts. Greg co-authored "The Collectors Estate Handbook," winner of the NLG's Robert Friedberg Award for numismatic book of the year. He previously served two terms on the seven-person Advisory Board to the Federal Reserve Bank of Dallas.

Adam Smith. *An Inquiry into the Nature and Causes of the Wealth of Nations.*
Sold for $125,000 | July 2022

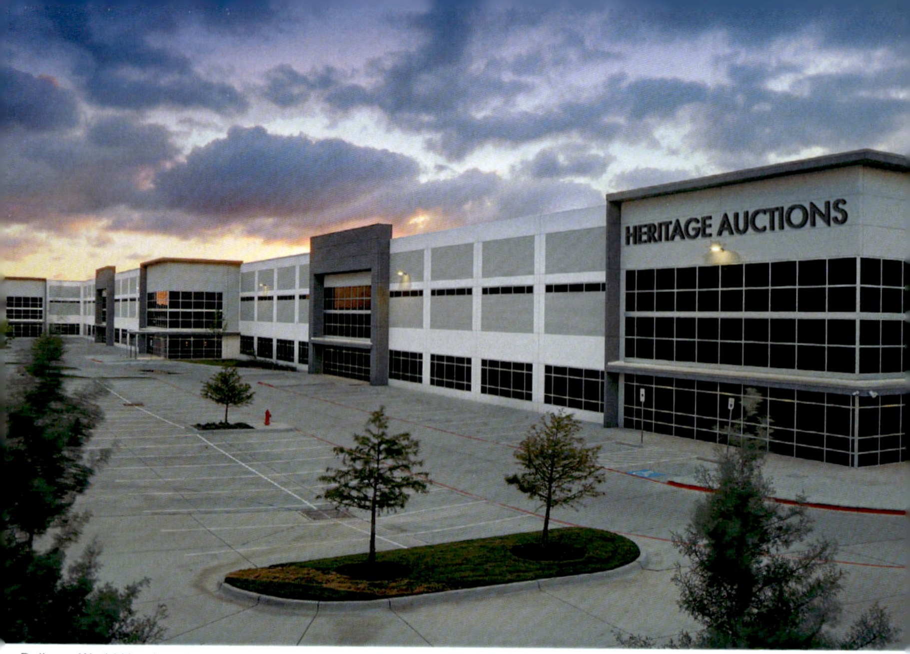

Dallas - World Headquarters

Beverly Hills

New York

Chicago

Palm Beach

Brussels

Amsterdam

London

Hong Kong

About Heritage Auctions

Founded in 1976, Heritage Auctions is America's auction house and the world's largest collectibles auctioneer with annual topping $1.45 billion in both 2021 and 2022. Heritage clients enjoy unprecedented access to 1.75 million+ online bidder members and unparalleled standards of honesty and transparency as well as the latest advancements in technology via HA.com.

Through 50+ categories – from U.S. and foreign coins to fine art and now luxury real estate auctions – Heritage Auctions offers a broad range of services for high net worth collectors, investors and fiduciaries from offices in Dallas, New York, Beverly Hills, Chicago, Palm Beach, London, Brussels, Paris, Amsterdam and Hong Kong.

Heritage Auctions offers consignors an unmatched depth of expertise with access to 6.1 million+ lots featured in Heritage Auctions' free Auction Archives and a network of 500+ specialist employees around the world.

We are always looking to acquire interesting items, whether through consignment or by outright purchase, and we spend or disburse millions of dollars every business day, on average, to keep our clients' demands satisfied. Find out why you should consign to a Heritage auction at HA.com/Consign.

Heritage Trusts & Estates Services

Individuals and collectors, as well as trustees, executors and fiduciaries responsible for estate tangible property, can avail themselves of the best suite of estate services anywhere, including authoritative estate appraisals, estate planning assistance, auction services and private treaty sales.

Inquiries: Michelle Castro, Vice President, Trust & Estates, 214-409-1824 or 877-HERITAGE (437-4824) ext. 1824, MichelleC@HA.com

Heritage Auctions Appraisal Services, Inc.

Heritage offers the highest caliber of experts to evaluate and appraise your art and collectibles. Working with our appraisal team, you will receive thorough, illustrated appraisal reports written in compliance with all IRS, USPAP and insurance standards. At competitive rates, a Heritage appraisal should be considered for all Estate Tax, Charitable Donation, Insurance, Estate or Financial Planning situations.

Inquiries: Carol Lee Pryor, Director of Appraisal Services, 214-409-1138 or 877-HERITAGE (437-4824) ext. 1138, CarolLeeP@HA.com

1966 Baseball Hall of Fame Induction Ring Presented to Ted Williams.
Sold for $444,000 | May 2023

HERITAGE
A U C T I O N S
AMERICA'S AUCTION HOUSE

DALLAS | NEW YORK | BEVERLY HILLS | CHICAGO | PALM BEACH

LONDON | HONGKONG | MUNICH | TOKYO | PARIS | AMSTERDAM | BRUSSELS | GENEVA

Always Accepting Quality Consignments in 50+ Categories

2 Million+ Online Bidder-Members

Tax Planning, Strategy and Estate Advice for Collectors and Their Heirs.

As a collector, you know your collection inside and out. But do your potential heirs? In clear, practical terms, industry veterans James L. Halperin and Gregory J. Rohan provide you with invaluable guidance on how to:

- Document your collection
- Safeguard your collection
- Evaluate your collection
- Sell your collection
- Minimize taxes upon transfer
- Make the most effective charitable gift
- Help your heirs ... and much more.

Completely revised and updated to include the most recent federal tax law changes and new information on collectibles and charitable planning, *The Collector's Handbook* will help you protect your investment. Whatever your motivations in collecting, this book will help make you a more intelligent collector.

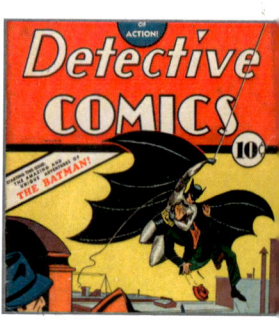

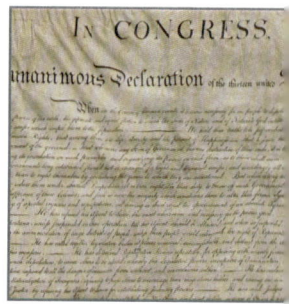

"When it comes to collectibles, no one knows more than the folks at Heritage."

– ANDREW TOBIAS
New York Times Bestselling Author of
The Only Investment Guide You'll Ever Need

88270

ISBN 978-1-63351-472-0

90000>

9 781633 514720